RECIPES AND FROM FAMILY AND FRIENDS

SANGEETA JOSHI

Copyright © Sangeeta Joshi
All Rights Reserved.

This book has been self-published with all reasonable efforts taken to make the material error-free by the author. No part of this book shall be used, reproduced in any manner whatsoever without written permission from the author, except in the case of brief quotations embodied in critical articles and reviews.

The Author of this book is solely responsible and liable for its content including but not limited to the views, representations, descriptions, statements, information, opinions and references ["Content"]. The Content of this book shall not constitute or be construed or deemed to reflect the opinion or expression of the Publisher or Editor. Neither the Publisher nor Editor endorse or approve the Content of this book or guarantee the reliability, accuracy or completeness of the Content published herein and do not make any representations or warranties of any kind, express or implied, including but not limited to the implied warranties of merchantability, fitness for a particular purpose. The Publisher and Editor shall not be liable whatsoever for any errors, omissions, whether such errors or omissions result from negligence, accident, or any other cause or claims for loss or damages of any kind, including without limitation, indirect or consequential loss or damage arising out of use, inability to use, or about the reliability, accuracy or sufficiency of the information contained in this book.

Made with ❤ on the Notion Press Platform
www.notionpress.com

To

Dattakiran Joshi

Divya Joshi

Shivani Joshi

For being by my side in this food journey

For tolerating my hits and misses

For all the encouragement

Contents

Foreword	xi
Acknowledgements	xiii
Introduction	xv

Soups, Salads And Raitas

1. Tomato Soup	3
2. Sweet Corn Soup	4
3. Spinach Soup	5
4. Raw Mango And Dal Salad	6
5. Koshimbir	7
6. Corn Capsicum Salad	10
7. Raw Papaya Salad	11
8. Three Bean Salad	12
9. Bread Salad	13
10. Bhindi Raita	14
11. Boondi Raita	15
12. Mint (Pudina) Raita	16
13. Mixed Vegetable Raita	17

Snacks

14. Batata Vada	21
15. Sabudana Vada	22
16. Sabudana Khichdi	23
17. Kothimbir Vadi	24
18. Paddu	25
19. Dhokla	26
20. Eaglenest Pakodas	28
21. Salted Cashews	29
22. Poha	30
23. Upma	31

Contents

24. Rava Idli	32
25. Aloo Sagu	33
26. Breads For Breakfast	34
27. Dosa	38
28. Aloo Sabji For Dosa Filling	40
29. Idli	41
30. Adai	42
31. Appam	43
32. Idiappam	44
33. Vegetable Stew	45
34. Tomato Omelette	46
35. Bhoplyache Gharge	47
36. Moong Dal Chillas	48
37. Vegetable Cutlet	49
38. Bhel Puri	50
39. Chaats	51
40. Dahi Vada	53
41. Stuffed Garlic Bread	55
42. Pav Bhaji	57
43. Matki Patal Bhaji	59
44. Kodubale	61
45. Poha Chiwda	62

Main Course

46. Avial	67
47. Vegetable Sagu	68
48. Cabbage Poriyal	69
49. Peeth Perun Capsicum	71
50. Corn Capsicum Sabji	72

Contents

51. Baingan Bharta	73
52. Cheese Baingan	74
53. Exotic Cauliflower	75
54. Lychee Kofta In Makhani Gravy	76
55. Navratan Korma	78
56. Paneer Bhurji	79
57. Sarson Ka Saag	80
58. Saucy Paneer	81
59. Vegetarian Shepherd's Pie	82
60. Stuffed Bhindi	84
61. Bhindi Do Pyaaza	85
62. Asian Stir Fried Vegetables	86

Dals And Liquid Accompaniments

63. Aamti	89
64. Tomato Saar	90
65. Cholar Dal	91
66. Maa Chole Di Dal	92
67. Sookhi Urad Dal	93
68. Tomato Rasam	94
69. Sambar	95
70. Mor Kuzhambu	97
71. Kabuli Chana	98
72. Sinful Punjabi Chole	100
73. Dalma	102

Rice

74. Types Of Rice Its Cooking Methods	105
75. Flavoured Rice	107
76. Curd Rice	109

Contents

77. Jeera Rice	110
78. Ven Pongal	111
79. Sweet Pongal	112
80. Vegetable Biryani	113
81. Bisibele Bhath	116

Breads

82. Puri And Luchi	121
83. Stuffed Paratha	123
84. Jowar Thalipeeth	127
85. Pangi	128
86. Thepla	129
87. Matar Kachori With Aloo Rassa	130
88. Aloo Kachori	132

Sweets And Desserts

89. Besan Ladoo	135
90. Chirote	136
91. Gajar Halwa	137
92. Shahi Tukda	138
93. Sooji Halwa (Sheera)	139
94. Shrikhand	140
95. Rice Kheer	141
96. Seviyan Kheer	142
97. Phirni	143
98. Modak	144
99. Kulfi	146
100. Mishti Doi	147
101. Bhappa Doi	149
102. Sandesh	150

Contents

103. Fruit Yoghurt	151
104. Vanilla Ice Cream	152
105. Mango Mastani	155
106. Chocolate Cake	156
107. Custard Chocolate Sauce Biscuit Pudding	157
108. Choco Lava Cake	159
109. Tiramisu	161
110. Apple Pie	162
Chutneys And Sauces	
111. Tomato Chutney (Bengali Style)	167
112. Aamer Chutney (Bengali Raw Mango Chutney)	168
113. Coconut Chutney	169
114. Coconut Coriander Chutney	170
115. Mint Coriander Chutney	171
116. Raw Mango And Mint Chutney	173
117. Red Dosa Chutney	174
118. Thokku	175
119. Dry Garlic Chutney	176
120. White Sauce (Béchamel Sauce)	177
Useful tips	179
Glossary	181

Foreword

There is no dearth of recipe books in the market, and nowadays almost everyone can be a YouTube chef. Why then, would someone want to publish a recipe book?

It was always said that if you ask a lady for a recipe, she would proudly share it but hold back one tiny little detail. Thankfully, we have been fortunate to have friends and family who didn't mind sharing their secrets wholeheartedly, leading to this compilation of seasoned and tested recipes. Each one has been validated by the author and improved after titration and experimentation on yours truly.

It was soon after her marriage that the author, who is a medical doctor, discovered that cooking for the family is a pleasure rather than a chore. The book is therefore based on a much thumbed and yellowed diary which she started maintaining since the time when Windows were openings in a wall.

The dishes are those which can be prepared in an average Indian house with commonly available ingredients. The instructions are lucid, and the narrative replete with anecdotes which is sure to impart a unique flavour to the recipes. The section on useful tips is especially noteworthy as it is borne from first-hand experience.

Being a vegetarian household, there was no scope to have a non-vegetarian section in the book. However, what lends variety is that cuisine from different parts of India is included, and many recipes owe their origins to faraway lands.

The book should appeal not only to those entering the kitchen for the first time, but also to those experienced cooks who are seekers of perfection in simple everyday recipes.

Dr. Dattakiran Joshi
(The fortunate husband)

Acknowledgements

- Late Mrs. Shakunthala Chellappa – my mother
- Mrs. Vijaya Joshi – my mother-in-law
- Late Mrs. Vasantha Raju – my aunt
- Late Mrs. Rajendra Sahai
- Smeeta Neogi
- Dr. Neelamani Murthy
- Indu Nair
- Mitali Nandi
- Dr. Anupama Devgan
- Meenaxi Bhatt
- Dr. Debmita Debdas
- Poonam Sandhu
- Dr. Wajiha Rehman
- Lakshmi Ramakrishnan
- Dr. Sandhya Khare
- Dr. Anagha Agrawal
- Deepa Rajagopal
- Sushma Indrajit
- Dr. Arti Chaturvedi
- Usha Vidyashankar
- Shanti Rupnarayan
- Deepti Karmarkar
- Dr. Manoshi Bhattacharya
- Dr. Chandreyee Bhattacharya
- Dr. Shivani Joshi
- Bandana Sahu
- Dr. Divya Joshi
- Rajani Kamat
- Uma Sridhar
- Maria Duckworth
- Rita Fernandez
- Ginderjeet Kaur Kang
- Dr. Ritweez Sahu
- Shyamali Chatterjee

Introduction

I enjoy cooking; and my family enjoys eating. My husband gives constructive criticism and my two daughters are game for anything new. I learnt the basics of South Indian food from my mother and even after so many years, I still feel I am not up to her level. I married into a Maharashtrian family and my mother-in-law inducted me into the nuances of Marathi food.

My interest in cooking started at a young age when my parents gave me the encouragement and freedom to experiment, first with the oven and then with the gas stove. They appreciated and gave advice to improve my skills. After completing my medical education, working and having two girls, cooking did take a back seat until the children started going to school. I remember my younger daughters' friend chiding me for repeating boring biscuits in the school snack box for 4 days. He used to surreptitiously partake of the tiffin and my daughter had to devise means of hiding it! And the unwritten rule at home was to never repeat the tiffin in a week – be it the savory or the sweet component. I think this spurred me to learn and create innovative tiffins.

Being from the armed forces, entertaining is an integral part of our lives. In every party, we end up tasting something new and as a corollary l learn a new recipe. My dining table has been a smorgasbord of dishes from all over India and few from our trips to foreign lands. There are hits and misses, but all said, this has been a fun journey and continues to remain so. My misses –Dr. Anagha's Rosogolla, Uma's rava dosa and pickles of all varieties.

This book is in Hinglish, and it echoes my family's dining table. I have tried to remain faithful to the recipes but have tweaked a step or two. The cup mentioned in the recipes holds 200 ml. We eat less spice at home, so the chilli and spice levels may have to be adjusted accordingly. Also, I believe in letting the inherent flavors of the vegetables and lentils come out. As against this, we all have a sweet tooth, and the desserts section may have to be tempered down. I use only sunflower oil for cooking, that too in moderation. Having said this, I have mentioned the names of certain store bought items and as far as possible I stick with these brands only.

My married daughters are also managing their own kitchens and I get many urgent calls when they are stuck at a certain step with a recipe. The idea behind writing this book stemmed from this, so they have a

INTRODUCTION

ready reckoner at hand. Ideal for beginners and for those who want to try out something new, my book may be a starting point. For those who believe in takeaways, frozen foods, and dining outs, don't shy away from your kitchen. Believe me, the pleasure you would derive eating your own creation is indescribable.

And last but not the least, my sincere thanks to Chef Sanjeev Kapoor and his show Khana Khazana. It is he who inspired me to step out of my comfort zone and move into unchartered territories. Thanks also to Neeta Mehta, Tarla Dalal, Ranveer Brar, Sanjyot Keer and MasterChef Australia, who keep the culinary fire in me burning even till date.

Dr. Sangeeta Joshi

Soups, Salads and Raitas

- Tomato Soup
- Sweet Corn Soup
- Spinach Soup
- Raw Mango and Dal Salad
- Koshimbir
- Corn Capsicum Salad
- Raw Papaya Salad
- Three Bean Salad
- Bread Salad
- Bhindi Raita
- Boondi Raita
- Mint Raita
- Mixed Vegetable Raita

Tomato Soup

(to serve 4)

Nothing beats this tomato soup on a wintry evening. It is so vibrant and fresh that I could have bowls of soup along with bread and a light salad alone for dinner.

Ingredients

- 4 tomatoes medium size
- 1 small carrot chopped
- 1 medium onion chopped
- ½ inch ginger chopped
- ½ tsp salt (or to taste)
- 2 tsp sugar
- ½ tsp freshly ground pepper

Method

1. Slit the tomatoes. Place the tomatoes, carrot, onion and ginger in a bowl and pressure cook it for 7-8 minutes.
2. Remove from the cooker and let cool.
3. Puree in a mixer and strain well.
4. Place the mixture in a pan on medium flame. Adjust the consistency with water as per your desire.
5. Add salt, sugar and pepper.
6. Bring to a boil and then simmer for 5 minutes. Check the seasoning. Serve hot.

For garnish (optional)

1. Grated cheese 2 tbsp
2. Or croutons made from toasted bread
3. Or swirl a tsp of beaten cream on top of each individual bowl of soup

Sweet Corn Soup

A favorite accompaniment to a Chinese dinner.

Ingredients

- 1 tin sweet corn cream style (400 gm)
- ½ tsp salt or to taste, ½ tsp pepper powder
- 1 tbsp cornflour

Method 1

1. Empty the tinned sweet corn into a pan.
2. Add 3 cups of water and stir till all the corn is uniformly mixed.
3. Add salt and pepper. Bring to a boil. Lower the flame.
4. Mix the cornflour with water to form a paste.
5. Add to the boiling corn mixture gradually, and mix well.
6. Simmer for 5 minutes. The soup should be thick in consistency.
7. Adjust the seasoning and the consistency of the soup. Serve hot.

Method 2

1. Instead of tinned sweet corn, use 2 fresh sweet corns.
2. Boil the corns in water. Separate the kernels.
3. Puree 2 tbsp sweet corn kernels with a little water.
4. Boil 2 cups of water. Add the sweet corn puree, salt, ½ tsp sugar, and pepper powder and bring to a boil.
5. Add the rest of the corn kernels. Simmer for 5 minutes.
6. Adjust the seasonings. Add the optional vegetables and spring onions. Serve hot.

Tips:

1. Beat one egg lightly. Add half the beaten egg to the hot soup when almost done, stirring all the while till you get thin strands.
2. Add the vegetables to the soup while it is boiling: 2 tbsp finely chopped carrot, 5 beans finely chopped, 2 tbsp finely chopped spring onion greens, 2 tbsp boiled sweet corn kernels.

Spinach Soup

A delicious winter soup when tender spinach floods the markets.

Ingredients

- Half kg spinach
- 1 large onion
- ½ tsp salt or to taste
- ¼ tsp fresh pepper powder
- 1 cup milk

Method:

1. Use only the leaves of the spinach. Wash in running water at least three times.
2. Meanwhile, boil water. Blanch the spinach in boiling water for 3 minutes. The leaves should retain the green color.
3. Drain well. Cool and puree finely.
4. Chop the onion and boil the onion in water for 5 minutes. Drain and grind the boiled onion into a paste.
5. Mix the purees with milk. Strain the puree mixture to get a smooth soup. Add salt and pepper.
6. Place in a thick-bottomed pan and boil on a medium flame for 4-5 minutes. Adjust the seasoning and the consistency of the soup with milk.
7. Serve hot.

Tips

1. Finely grate 2-inch slice of paneer and add to the soup before serving.
2. Top with grated cheese.

Raw Mango and Dal Salad

A typical Maharashtrian accompaniment – as a chutney or salad, especially in summers when raw mangoes are plentiful.

Ingredients

- ½ cup channa dal, soaked for 3-4 hours
- ¼ cup grated raw mango
- 1 green chilli
- 2 tbsp grated coconut
- 2 tbsp coriander leaves
- ¼ tsp sugar
- Salt to taste

For tempering

- 1 tsp oil
- ¼ tsp mustard seeds
- Pinch of hing
- 5 curry leaves

Method

1. Grind the soaked dal with the green chilli coarsely.
2. Add the raw mango, coconut, coriander leaves, salt and sugar.
3. Mix well.
4. Heat the oil well.
5. Add mustard seeds and fry till they crackle.
6. Add curry leaves and hing.
7. Pour over the dal mixture. Mix well and serve cold.

Koshimbir

This is a typical Maharashtrian salad had with everyday meals.

Cucumber Koshimbir

Ingredients

- 1 medium cucumber
- 2 tbsp coarsely ground roasted peanuts
- 1 finely chopped green chilli
- 1 tbsp coriander leaves, chopped
- ½ tsp sugar
- Salt to taste
- 3 tbsp curd

Method

1. Peel the cucumber and grate with the larger side of grater.
2. Add half tsp salt and keep aside for 15 to 20 minutes.
3. Squeeze out the excess water.
4. Add 2 tbsp coarsely ground groundnut powder, sugar, green chilli, and coriander leaves. Mix well.
5. Add curd and mix. Adjust salt. And serve immediately.

• • •

Tomato Koshimbir

The procedure is the same as cucumber Koshimbir. The cucumber is replaced with 1 cup of finely chopped tomatoes.

• • •

Carrot Koshimbir

Ingredients

- 2 medium carrots peeled and grated
- 2 tbsp coarsely ground roasted peanuts
- 1 finely chopped green chilli
- 1 tbsp coriander leaves, chopped
- 1 tsp sugar
- Salt to taste
- 1 tbsp lime juice

Method

1. Mix all the above ingredients. And serve immediately

• • •

Cabbage Koshimbir

Ingredients

- 1 small cabbage grated
- 2 tbsp coarsely ground roasted peanuts
- 1 finely chopped green chilli
- 1 tbsp coriander leaves, chopped
- 1 tsp sugar
- Salt to taste
- 1 tbsp lime juice

Method

1. Mix all the above ingredients. And serve immediately

• • •

Banana Koshimbir

Ingredients

- 2 ripe bananas sliced
- Salt to taste
- 1 green chilli finely chopped or crushed
- 1 tbsp coriander leaves chopped
- ¼ tsp sugar
- 1 cup curd

Method

1. Mix the bananas, salt, sugar green chilli and coriander leaves.
2. Add curd and mix well.
3. Serve chilled.

Tip

1. I always keep roasted and coarsely ground peanuts readily available. The peanuts are roasted on a low flame till brown black specks appear on the skin. After the groundnuts are cool, the skin is peeled.
2. The groundnuts are ground coarsely, cooled and stored. This keeps for a week and remains fresh.

Corn Capsicum Salad

A light salad to be had especially in summers when sweet corns are available in plenty.

Ingredients

- 2 small sweet corns- boiled and kernels taken out
- Red, yellow, green capsicum – half each. Diced.
- ½ cup spring onion greens chopped into ½ cm pieces
- ½ tsp freshly ground pepper
- Salt to taste
- 1 tbsp lemon juice or vinegar
- ½ tsp powdered sugar
- 1 tsp olive oil

Method:

1. Mix the lemon juice, olive oil, sugar, salt and pepper well. (I keep a small empty glass bottle with lid for this. I add the ingredients and give a good shake).
2. Mix the corn kernels, capsicums and spring onion greens. Add the dressing and toss well. Serve cold.

Tip

1. I usually add the dressing 10 minutes before serving.

Raw Papaya Salad

Another summer favorite of mine when raw mangoes and raw papayas are easily available.

Ingredients

- 1 small raw papaya
- 1 medium cucumber
- 1 medium raw mango
- 1 small carrot
- 1 tbsp lemon juice
- Salt to taste
- ½ tsp powdered sugar or 1 tsp honey
- ½ tsp pepper powder
- 1 tsp olive oil
- 2 tbsp roasted and coarsely crushed peanuts
- A few sprigs of coriander for garnish

Method

1. Peel and julienne the raw papaya, cucumber, raw mango and carrot into very thin strips – 2 inches long.
2. Toss them in a serving bowl.
3. Mix the lemon juice, salt, sugar, pepper and oil in a small bowl.
4. Pour over the salad and mix well.
5. Add the peanuts and mix.
6. Garnish with coriander leaves and serve chilled.

Three Bean Salad

A protein rich salad, made colorful by the tomatoes, spring onion greens.

Ingredients:

- Rajma half cup soaked overnight
- Kabuli channa half cup soaked overnight
- Kala channa half cup soaked overnight
- Lobia half cup soaked for 2 hours (optional)
- Salt ½ tsp
- Chaat masala 1 tsp
- Lemon juice 1 tbsp
- Coriander leaves chopped 2 tbsp
- Green chilli 1 finely chopped
- Spring onion – 3 stalks – greens and bulb chopped finely (optional)

Method:

1. Rinse the soaked beans well and boil separately. Rajma and Kabuli channa will take 20 minutes after the whistle, while kala channa will take 40 minutes after the cooker whistle. Lobia takes 10 minutes in the cooker. However, check with your cooker settings and performance and adjust the time accordingly. The beans should be cooked but not mushy.
2. Mix all the cooked beans in a serving bowl. Add the rest of the ingredients. Chill and serve cold.

Tips

1. You could add 1 medium onion finely chopped and 1 medium tomato deseeded and finely chopped, to give added flavour and taste.

Bread Salad

Mrs. Shanti Rupnarayan used to make this delicious salad and the simplicity of preparation made it our house favorite.

Ingredients

- 1 loaf bakery bread cut into thick slices not wholly, but leaving the slices attached at the base
- 1 ½ cups cream
- ¼ tsp salt or to taste
- ½ tsp freshly ground pepper
- 1 tsp olive oil
- 1 tsp powdered sugar
- Half carrot peeled and shredded or julienned
- ½ cup shredded cabbage
- Half green capsicum julienned
- Juice of 1 lemon

Method

1. Mix the cream, salt, sugar, pepper, oil and lemon juice in a bowl. Add the shredded carrot, cabbage and capsicum to it.
2. Place the bread loaf on a plate and open the slices.
3. Pour the cream mixture over the bread and in between the slices.
4. Chill and serve.

Bhindi Raita

A different way to use bhindi. The crunch of the bhindis adds to the texture of the raita.

Ingredients

- Bhindi 100 gm
- Curd 500 ml
- ½ tsp salt or to taste
- 2 tbsp oil for frying the bhindi
- For tempering
- 1 tsp oil
- 2 red chillies
- ½ tsp mustard seeds
- Pinch hing

Method

1. Wash and dry the bhindi thoroughly.
2. Chop the bhindi finely (4 mm thick).
3. Heat 2 tbsp oil in a pan and fry the bhindi till they are golden brown.
4. Remove and drain on a kitchen towel.
5. Beat curd with salt and keep aside.

For tempering:

1. Heat 1 tsp oil.
2. Add mustard seeds and fry till they crackle.
3. Add the red chilli and fry for 1 minute.
4. Put off the gas and add the hing.
5. Pour the tempering over the beaten curd.
6. Just before serving add the bhindi.
7. Adjust salt if required.
8. Serve with pulao or Bisibele Bhath.

Boondi Raita

I use store bought boondi for the raita. Each brand has a different time to turn soft. So do try out a small amount first before standardizing the time.

Ingredients

- 1 cup boondi – store bought
- 500 ml thick curd
- ½ tsp salt or to taste
- 1 tsp roasted jeera powder
- ½ tsp red chilli powder
- ½ tsp kala namak

Method

1. Take the boondi in a bowl. Pour half litre of hot water over it. Keep aside for 3 minutes.
2. Drain the boondi in a sieve. Cool.
3. Beat the curd till smooth.
4. Add the salt, kala namak, roasted jeera powder and red chilli powder to the beaten curd and mix well.
5. Add the boondi to the beaten curd and mix well.
6. Serve chilled.

Mint (Pudina) Raita

A refreshing summer raita when mint leaves are so fresh and tender.

Ingredients

- 1 cup pudina leaves without stalks
- 1 green chilli
- 500 ml curd
- ½ tsp salt
- ½ tsp kala namak
- 2 tsp powdered sugar

Method

1. Rinse the pudina leaves in water at least three times.
2. Grind along with one green chilli and 1 tbsp curd to a fine paste.
3. Beat the curd till smooth.
4. Add the salt, kala namak, powdered sugar and pudina paste to the curd. Mix well. Adjust salt and seasonings.
5. Serve chilled.

Tips

1. You may add 1 boiled potato (finely diced) to the raita. This gives a texture and body to the raita.

Mixed Vegetable Raita

A standard raita used as an accompaniment to pulao, biryani, paratha etc

Ingredients

- 500 ml thick curd
- ½ tsp salt or to taste
- ¼ tsp kala namak
- ½ tsp chaat masala
- Half cup each of finely diced cucumber, deseeded tomato, finely chopped onion
- 1 green chilli finely chopped
- 2 tbsp finely chopped coriander leaves

Method

1. Beat the curd till it is smooth.
2. Add the salt, kala namak and chaat masala.
3. Add the vegetables 10 minutes before serving (or else the curd gets diluted with the water from the vegetables).
4. Garnish with coriander and serve chilled.

Snacks

- Batata Vada
- Sabudana Vada
- Sabudana Khichdi
- Kothimbir Vadi
- Paddu
- Dhokla
- Eagle Nest Pakodas
- Salted Cashews
- Poha
- Upma
- Rava idli
- Aloo Sagu
- Breads for Breakfast
- Dosa
- Idli
- Adai
- Appam
- Idiappam
- Vegetable Stew
- Tomato Omelette
- Bhoplyachi Gharge
- Moong Dal Chillas
- Vegetable Cutlet
- Bhel Puri
- Chaats
- Dahi Vada
- Stuffed Garlic Bread
- Pav Bhaji
- Matki Patal Bhaji
- Kodubale
- Poha Chiwda

Batata Vada

(Makes 12)

An eternal favorite street food of Maharashtra. Served by itself or between slices of pav with dry garlic chutney.

Ingredients
For filling

- 5 medium potatoes boiled
- 2 tbsp finely chopped coriander leaves
- 4 garlic cloves peeled and chopped
- 2 green chillies chopped
- 1 inch ginger chopped
- 1 tbsp oil
- Salt to taste
- Juice of 2 lemons

For Batter

- 1 cup besan (Coarse –mota- besan if available gives best results)
- ¼ tsp salt, ¼ tsp cooking soda
- Pinch of hing
- Oil for frying

Method

1. Cool and peel the potatoes. Dice the potatoes into small cubes. Do not mash.
2. Spread the potatoes on a plate. Add salt, 2 tbsp finely chopped coriander leaves.
3. Pound the garlic, ginger and chilli together.
4. Heat 1 tbsp oil. Add the garlic-chilli-ginger mixture and fry for one minute. Add this oil and fried mixture to the potato. Add juice of 2 lemons to the potatoes. Mix well with hand. Make lemon sized balls.
5. While the potatoes are boiling, take 1 cup besan in a bowl. Add salt, soda, hing, and mix. Add water to make a thick batter. Keep aside for half an hour.
6. Heat oil for frying in a kadhai. Whisk the besan batter well to aerate it.
7. Dip each ball in besan batter and deep fry on medium heat till light golden in colour.
8. Drain on a kitchen towel and serve with mint chutney or dry garlic chutney.

Sabudana Vada

(makes 15 small vadas)

A popular snack at our house, especially when I feel indulgent.

Ingredients

- 1 cup sabudana
- 3 tbsp roasted and crushed ground nuts (can be done earlier)
- 1 large potato boiled and diced into small pieces
- 2 green chillies chopped
- 2 tsp sugar
- Salt to taste
- 1 tbsp chopped coriander
- Juice of 1 lime
- Oil for deep frying

Method

1. Soak the sabudana in just enough water to cover it, for 2 to 3 hours at least. I usually keep it overnight.
2. Mix the sabudana with the groundnut, potatoes, green chilli, salt, sugar, coriander leaves and lime juice.
3. Mix well and make around 15 balls from the mixture. Flatten them slightly.
4. Meanwhile, heat oil in a kadhai. The oil should be medium hot.
5. Put one ball in the oil. See that it doesn't separate or burst.
6. Fry the balls till golden brown.
7. Remove and drain on a kitchen towel to drain off the excess oil.
8. Serve hot with coconut or mint chutney or tomato sauce.

Tips

1. Some sabudana brands cook better when soaked overnight.
2. Do not roll the balls tightly. They are sure to burst.
3. Do not mash the potato. Keeping it diced allows for space for the sabudana to expand and reduces chances of bursting.

Sabudana Khichdi

An eternal favourite at our house. We could have it for breakfast, lunch and dinner. This is my mother-in-laws recipe.

Ingredients (to serve 2)

- 1 cup sabudana
- 3 tbsp roasted and crushed groundnuts (can be done earlier and stored)
- 1 medium potato – chopped into 1 cm pieces
- 1 tsp jeera
- 2 green chillies slit
- 2 tsp sugar
- Salt to taste
- 3 tbsp ghee
- 1 tbsp chopped coriander for garnish
- 1 tbsp grated coconut for garnish

Method

1. Soak the sabudana in just enough water to cover it, for 2 to 3 hours. I usually soak it overnight.
2. Heat a kadhai or a heavy bottom pan. Add the ghee.
3. Once heated, add the jeera. Once it sizzles add the slit green chillies.
4. Fry for 1 minute and then add the potatoes. Cover and cook in low flame for 3-4 minutes or until the potatoes are done.
5. While the potatoes are cooking, mix the sabudana with the crushed groundnut, salt and sugar.
6. Once potatoes are done, add in the sabudana mixture. Mix thoroughly. Cover and cook in low flame for 4-5 minutes stirring once or twice in between.
7. Once done, the sabudana pearls will appear translucent. Put off the gas.
8. Garnish with coriander leaves and coconut.
9. Enjoy with a slice of lemon or curd.

Kothimbir Vadi

Kothimbir Vadi – this is inspired by a relative's recipe of cabbage vadi and Ranveer Brar's recipe

Ingredients

- 2 cups chopped dhania leaves
- 1 cup besan
- 2 tbsp rice powder
- 1 tsp ginger-green chilli paste
- 1 tsp jeera powder
- ¼ tsp cooking soda
- 1 tsp powdered jaggery
- 1 tsp imli pulp or amchur
- ½ tsp sesame seeds
- Salt to taste
- Oil for frying

Method

1. Grease a plate with oil and keep aside.
2. Boil water in a pressure cooker with the whistle removed or in a steamer.
3. Mix all the above in a bowl. Add water to make a thick batter.
4. Pour the batter on the greased plate about an inch thick.
5. Steam for 15 minutes. Remove from steamer and sprinkle sesame seeds on top. Press lightly. Cool.
6. Cut into pieces.
7. You could deep fry the pieces or shallow fry or fry in the air fryer.
8. Serve with pudina chutney.

Tips:

1. You could add 1 cup grated cabbage and 1 cup chopped coriander leaves to the above mixture to make Kobi vadi

Paddu

This is an ideal party snack, so easy to make and versatile.

Ingredients (makes 12)

- Dosa batter 2 cups (salted)
- 1 medium Onion finely chopped
- 2 tbsp coriander leaves, finely chopped
- 1 green chilli, finely chopped
- Oil for greasing the appe pan

Method

1. Mix all of the above except the oil.
2. Heat the appe pan after greasing with oil.
3. Put one tbsp of the batter in each mould of the pan.
4. Cover and cook on medium heat for 3 minutes.
5. Open the lid and turn the paddus around to cook the bottom side.
6. Cover and cook for 2 minutes.
7. Remove on a plate.
8. Serve warm, along with coconut chutney.

Dhokla

(Makes 8 pieces)

This is an instant dhokla, which does not require fermenting. Can be made within half an hour when surprise guests arrive.

Ingredients

- 1 cup besan
- 1 tsp sooji
- Salt to taste
- 2 tsp powdered sugar
- Juice of 1 medium lemon
- 1 tsp ginger green chilli paste
- ¾ tsp cooking soda or 1 sachet of Eno (5 gm)

For tadka

- 1 tsp oil
- ½ tsp rai
- ½ tsp white til
- Pinch of hing
- 2 green chillies slit

Garnish

- 1 tbsp chopped coriander leaves
- 1 tbsp grated coconut

Method

1. Firstly keep steam ready - either in the cooker or a steamer.
2. Sieve besan. Add all ingredients for dhokla except soda. Grease a pan with oil and keep ready.
3. When the steam starts coming, add soda/ Eno to the besan mix. Mix. Add 2/3 cup water. Mix well in a circular motion gently. You will see the mixture rise.

4. Immediately pour the batter in the greased dish and steam for 10-12 minutes. Cool.
5. Tadka - heat oil. Add rai, til, hing and green chillies. Put of the heat. Add half a cup of water. Let it rest for 5 minutes.
6. Take out the pan with dhokla. Add the tadka (with water). Let it absorb completely.
7. Cut into squares and garnish with coriander leaves and coconut. Serve with green chutney.

Eaglenest Pakodas

While on a birding trip to Eaglenest Bird Sanctuary in Arunachal Pradesh, after a splendid mornings birding session, we were treated to these pakodas. Having them with a cup of tea, in the biting cold, made us thankful for these little pleasures in life.

Ingredients

- Bread slices 5 (2 -3 days old) cut roughly into pieces
- 1 carrot grated
- ½ capsicum grated
- ¼ small cabbage finely sliced
- 2 inch cheese block, grated
- ½ tsp salt
- ½ tsp pepper powder
- Water to bind
- Oil for frying

Method

1. Mix all the above ingredients except water and oil.
2. Add enough water to bind the mixture so that you can pat into small flat balls.
3. Heat the oil.
4. Fry the above balls over medium heat till brown.
5. Serve hot with sauce or mint chutney.

Salted Cashews

My friend Uma Sridhar always had these perfectly salted golden brown cashews for evening tea. And I learned what now looks like such a simple recipe. The trick here is to be patient and not hurry.

Ingredients:

- 2 cups whole cashewnuts
- 1 cup salt

Method:

1. Spread the salt in a flat frying pan.
2. Keep the pan on a low flame.
3. Add the cashews to the pan.
4. Keep stirring till you get a pale golden or light brown colour. This is where your patience pays.
5. Remove from heat. Cool.
6. Place it on a sieve to remove the salt.
7. You can reuse the salt for cooking.
8. Store the salted cashews in an airtight container.

Poha

(to serve 4)

An all-time Maharashtrian breakfast favorite at our house.

Ingredients

- 2 cups poha
- 1 onion chopped, 2 green chillies chopped
- 2 potatoes – chopped thinly into 1 cm pieces
- 2 tbsp green peas – boiled
- 2 tbsp groundnuts
- 2 tbsp coriander leaves chopped, 2 tbsp grated coconut for garnish
- 10 curry leaves
- 1 lime quartered
- ¼ tsp hing, ½ tsp haldi
- ¾ tsp salt or to taste
- 1 tsp sugar
- ¼ tsp mustard seeds, ¼ tsp jeera
- 3 tbsp oil

Method:

1. Take the poha in a bowl. Wash it with water. Drain, cover, and keep aside for 5 minutes. Heat oil in a frying pan. Add the groundnuts and fry till brown. Remove and keep aside.
2. Add the mustard seeds, jeera, hing and haldi to the oil. Fry for 15 seconds till the mustard seeds crackle. Add the curry leaves and green chillies. Add onion and fry till onion turns translucent.
3. Add the potato, cover and cook till the potatoes are soft and done.
4. Add poha, green peas, fried groundnuts, salt and sugar. Mix well and cook for 3 minutes over a low flame.
5. Garnish with coriander leaves and grated coconut. Serve hot with a wedge of nimbu.

Tips

1. To save time, my daughter Divya, keeps a boiled potato ready and adds diced boiled potatoes while making poha.

Upma

(serves 4)

A tiffin box special and a breakfast dish. To make it more colourful and appetizing, I sometimes add finely chopped carrots, French beans, potatoes and boiled green peas about 1 tbsp each at the frying stage.

Ingredients

- 1 cup sooji / rava
- 1 medium onion chopped finely
- 1 small capsicum, chopped finely
- 1 green chilli slit
- 2 tbsp coriander leaves
- 10 curry leaves
- Half inch ginger, grated
- ¼ tsp mustard seeds
- ½ tsp salt or to taste
- ½ tsp sugar
- 2 tbsp oil + 1 tsp oil
- 1 tsp ghee
- 2 ½ cups water

Method:

1. Heat 1 tsp oil. Add the sooji and roast it for at least 4-5 minutes on low flame. The colour should not change but may become a very light brown. Remove the sooji on a plate.
2. Add the remaining 2 tsp oil. Temper with mustard seeds, curry leaves and green chilli.
3. Add the onions and fry till the onions turn translucent. Add the capsicum and ginger and cook for 2 minutes. Optionally, you could also add different vegetables at this stage as mentioned above.
4. Add the water and bring it to a boil. Add salt, sugar and ghee. Reduce the flame and gradually mix in the roasted sooji.
5. Keep stirring. The mixture will gradually thicken and become slightly dry.
6. Remove from flame. Garnish with coriander leaves and serve hot.

Rava Idli

(makes 10)

The first time we went to my aunt Vasantha Raju's house at Indiranagar, Bangalore, she quickly went into the kitchen and made these instant rava idlis.

Ingredients

- 1 cup sooji
- 2 tsp oil
- ½ tsp salt or to taste
- 1 sachet Eno (5 gm) or can use ½ tsp cooking soda
- 5 curry leaves
- 3 tbsp chopped coriander leaves
- ½ tsp mustard seeds
- 1 tsp urad dal
- 1 ½ cup curd beaten
- 1 onion finely chopped, 1 green chilli finely chopped
- 2 tbsp finely chopped cabbage (optional)
- 1 tsp ghee, 8-10 broken cashews

Method:

1. Heat 1 tsp oil in a pan. Add sooji and roast it on a low flame for 3-4 minutes. Take out in a dish.
2. Add 1 cup curd, coriander leaves, salt, onion, cabbage and green chilli. Mix well and keep covered for 20 minutes.
3. In the meantime, heat an idli steamer or cooker with water. Heat till steam rises.
4. Take a tadka pan. Heat ghee and remaining 1 tsp oil and fry the cashews till golden. Remove the cashews in the sooji curd mixture.
5. To the remaining ghee-oil, add mustard seeds and urad dal. Fry till the dal is light brown and the mustard seeds crackle. Add to the sooji curd mixture. Grease the idli moulds with oil and keep ready.
6. Add the remaining curd to the above mixture along with the Eno/ cooking soda. Mix well. You may add more curd till a thick batter is obtained. Ladle into the idli moulds.
7. Steam for 12 to 14 minutes. Put off the gas and let it rest for 3 minutes before removing. Demould and serve hot with coconut chutney and aloo sagu.

Aloo Sagu

My aunt Vasantha Raju used to make this delicious aloo sagu which was served with rava idli.

Ingredients

- 3 potatoes
- 1 green chilli chopped
- 2 tbsp chopped coriander
- 2 tsp grated ginger
- 1 onion finely chopped
- 1 tomato finely chopped
- 10 curry leaves
- 2 tsp besan (gram flour)
- Salt to taste
- 1 tsp urad dal
- 2 tsp oil
- ½ tsp haldi
- Pinch of hing
- ½ tsp mustard seeds

Method:

1. Boil the potatoes till soft. Cool and crumble with hand
2. Heat oil in a pan. Add mustard seeds. Once they crackle, add hing, curry leaves, and urad dal. Sauté till the dal turns golden.
3. Add onions and sauté till translucent. Add tomatoes, green chili and ginger. Cook till the tomatoes are soft.
4. Add hing and haldi. Mix well and sauté for 2 minutes. Add besan. Sauté for a minute.
5. Add 1 cup of water and bring the mixture to a boil. Add the potatoes, and salt. Cover. Simmer for 8 minutes till the mixture thickens. Adjust the water till you get a thick curry.
6. Add the coriander leaves and switch off the gas. Serve with Rava Idli or Puri.

Breads for Breakfast

Our whole family loves bread. Be it cold sandwiches or grilled or toasted.
Cold sandwich: *A summer favorite*

1. Take 2 bread slices with edges off.
2. Spread butter on each.
3. Place 4 thinly sliced tomatoes, 3 thinly sliced cucumbers on one side. Sprinkle pepper.
4. Put a cheese slice on top. Dot with tomato sauce. Cover with the other slice.
5. Cut in two, keep covered with a moist kitchen towel and serve cold.

• • •

Chilli cheese toast:

1. Make a mixture with finely chopped green capsicum (half), finely chopped onions (1 small). Add 3 tbsp malai and 2 tbsp grated cheese and freshly ground pepper.
2. Spread on 2 bread slices and toast in an oven till the cheese melts and turns slightly brown.
3. Serve it hot.

• • •

Chutney sandwich:

1. Make green chutney either with raw mango or lemon (refer to the chutney section).
2. Take 2 slices of bread with edges removed.
3. Butter both slices lightly.
4. Spread green chutney on one side, and tomato sauce on the other side.
5. Place thinly sliced tomatoes and cucumbers on the chutney side. Place one cheese slice on it. Cover with the other slice. Cut in two. Keep covered with a moist cloth and serve cold.
6. Or you can grill it and serve hot.

• • •

VT sandwich:

This sandwich brings back memories of street food opposite the VT station in Mumbai (now called CST).

1. It is similar to the chutney sandwich as mentioned above. Add thinly sliced boiled potatoes, slivers of beetroot and onion in addition to the tomato and cucumbers. The spicier the green chutney, the more enjoyable it is.

• • •

Bread pakoda:

My husband's childhood favorite. I make it for him on a wet rainy day in the evenings along with a cup of steaming coffee or tea.

Ingredients

- 1 potato boiled and mashed, Salt to taste, Chaat masala
- Imli chutney, green chutney
- Oil for frying

Batter:

- 1 cup besan
- ¼ tsp salt
- pinch of cooking soda

Mix with water till you get a thick batter. Keep aside for 20 to 30 minutes.

Method

1. Boil 1 potato. Mash well till smooth. Add salt to taste, pinch of chaat masala. Keep aside.
2. Heat oil in a frying pan.
3. Place two slices of bread on top of each other. Cut into 2 halves to form two triangles.
4. Once the oil is hot, dip the triangles (with 2 slices) in the batter. Deep fry till golden.
5. Remove and drain on a kitchen towel.
6. Slit the long side of the triangle. Spread green chutney on one side, imli chutney on the other half and stuff with 1 tbsp of the mashed potato. Serve this sinful treat hot.

• • •

Bread upma:

Ingredients

- Stale (1 or 2 days old) bread 3 slices. Break roughly with the fingers into bite sized pieces.
- 1 onion finely chopped
- 1 tbsp coriander leaves chopped
- 1 green chilli chopped.
- 5 curry leaves
- ½ tsp mustard seeds
- ½ tsp haldi
- Pinch of hing
- Salt to taste
- 1 tbsp buttermilk
- Salt to taste
- 2 tbsp oil

Method

1. Heat the oil in a pan. Temper with mustard seeds, haldi and hing. Add the curry leaves and green chilli. Stir. Add the onions and sauté till the onions turn soft.
2. Add the bread and stir fry till well mixed. Add 1 tbsp butter milk. Add salt. Mix well.
3. Garnish with coriander leaves. Serve hot.

• • •

Bombay toast:

A favorite tiffin dabba snack for my kids while in school. I use the non-stick sandwich maker for this.

1. Butter both sides of 2 slices of bread. For filling, use grated cheese, chopped tomato, pepper powder, oregano or mixed Italian spice. Cover with the other slice and cook in the toaster for 3 minutes. The time will vary with each toaster. Also note that the first toast takes longer. Serve hot.

• • •

Corn spinach sandwich

1. Use the white sauce from the section on chutneys and sauces.

2. Take 10 leaves of spinach and blanch in boiling water for 2 minutes. Drain well and squeeze to remove all the water. Chop the spinach finely.
3. Boil 1 sweet corn and remove the kernels.
4. Mix the corn kernels, chopped spinach and 3 tbsp of white sauce.
5. Use this as a filling between two slices of bread. Serve cold.

•••

Mayonnaise and vegetable sandwich:

I use store-bought vegetarian mayonnaise for this. This can be made with regular mayonnaise also.

1. Peel and grate half a carrot. Finely chop a small piece of cabbage into thin strips.
2. Finely slice ¼ capsicum. Mix all the vegetables with 3 tbsp of mayonnaise.
3. Add ¼ tsp pepper powder.
4. Use this as a filling for a sandwich. Serve cold.

Dosa

After many trial and errors and various tips, I found that the following proportions gives the best results for a golden dosa. I get the best results with the dosa grinder which is an invaluable companion in my kitchen. Addition of the poha results in a golden brown crispy dosa, as was suggested by my friend Dr.Neelamani.

Ingredients

- 2 cups dosa rice
- 2 cups parboiled rice
- Half a cup poha
- 1 cup whole urad without skin
- 1 tbsp arhar dal
- ½ tsp methi seeds
- ½ tsp salt

Method:

1. Wash and soak both the rice together in water. Soak the poha separately in water.
2. Wash and soak the dals together.
3. Soak the methi seeds in half a cup of water.
4. All the above must be soaked for 6-8 hours.
5. In a dosa grinder – first grind the dals with methi with minimum water. Keep mixing in between and add water if required. At the end of 10 minutes, you should get a glossy white dal paste.
6. Remove in a large vessel.
7. Grind the rice and poha in a grinder till you get a smooth paste. This will take approximately 10-15 minutes.
8. Add the rice batter to the dal batter. Add salt. The batter should be like a thick cake batter (not runny).
9. Mix well by hand, adding water till you get a thick pouring consistency. Cover and keep aside in a warm place for 6-8 hours or overnight.

Preparation of dosa
Ingredients

- Dosa batter as above

- 1 onion cut in half
- Oil for cooking

Method:

1. Heat a non-stick or dosa tawa.
2. To check the heat, sprinkle a bit of water on the tawa. It should just sizzle. If it has become too hot, then reduce the flame and wait for a minute or two.
3. Put ¼ tsp oil on the tawa and spread all over the tawa with a cut onion.
4. Keep on low flame.
5. Add a ladleful of dosa batter in the centre. Spread in concentric circles outward with the back of the ladle till you get a thin dosa.
6. Increase the flame to medium high.
7. Cook till the sides of the dosa start leaving the tawa.
8. Fold the dosa and serve hot with chutney and sambar.

Tips

1. For masala dosa, add 1 tbsp of the aloo filling on the dosa, spread and then fold.
2. In winters, fermentation of the dosa may take longer. It is better to cover the vessel with a thick cloth (or old shawl) and keep in a cupboard.
3. If storing the remaining batter in the fridge, then the initial batter consistency should be just right. If it is too thick, it loses the bubbles and the dosa comes out flat the next day.

Aloo Sabji for Dosa Filling

Ingredients

- 3 potatoes – boiled and coarsely crumbled with hands
- 2 medium onions chopped
- ½ inch ginger - chopped fine
- 2 green chillies chopped
- 8-10 curry leaves
- 3 tbsp oil
- ½ tsp salt or to taste
- ½ tsp mustard seeds
- ½ tsp haldi
- 1 tsp urad dal

Method

1. Heat the oil in a pan. Add mustard seeds and fry till they crackle. Add the urad dal and fry till light brown. Add the curry leaves, green chillies, ginger and haldi. Stir for 1 minute on low flame.
2. Add the onions and sauté till pink. Add the boiled potatoes and salt.
3. Mix well. If it appears too dry add 2-3 tbsp of water. Cook on low flame for 5-6 minutes.
4. This is used as a stuffing for masala dosas.

Idli

My mother and I share a common liking – steaming hot idlis dunked in sambar. After many hits and trials, I got the following proportions to make silky soft idlis.

Ingredients:

- 3 cups idli rava or idli sooji
- 1 cup whole urad dal
- ½ tsp methi seeds
- Salt to taste
- Oil for greasing idli moulds

Method:

1. Soak the idli rava in adequate water overnight. Wash and soak the dal overnight in a separate vessel.
2. Soak the methi seeds in 2 tbsp water overnight.
3. Drain the urad dal. Grind the dal and methi in a grinder with minimum water till white and glossy. This should take 10 minutes. Remove in a vessel.
4. Drain the water from the idli rava. Take a fistful of the soaked rava and squeeze out the excess water. Add to the ground dal. Repeat till all the idli rava is added. Add salt.
5. Adjust the batter consistency with little water. The batter should be thicker than a dosa batter.
6. Keep covered in a warm place for 6-8 hours till fermented.

To make idlis:

1. In an idli steamer or cooker add 3 cups water and bring to a boil.
2. In the meantime, lightly grease the idli moulds with oil.
3. Pour a ladle full of idli batter in each mould.
4. Once the water is boiling, place the moulds in the steamer.
5. Lower the flame to medium and steam for 12-15 minutes.
6. Put off the gas and let it rest for 3 minutes.
7. With a spoon, remove the idlis and serve hot with chutney and sambar.

Adai

A protein packed dosa variety which does not need fermentation. This was made weekly at my mother's house.

Ingredients

- ¼ cup arhar dal
- ¼ cup urad dal (dhuli)
- ¼ cup moong dal (dhuli)
- ¼ cup channa dal
- 1 cup dosa rice
- 3 red chillies
- Salt ½ tsp or to taste
- ¼ tsp hing
- Oil for tava frying

Method

1. Soak the dals, rice and red chillies separately for 6 to 8 hours.
2. Grind them together till you get a coarse batter. Some people prefer a fine batter.
3. Add salt and hing.
4. Let it rest for at least 30 minutes (two to three hours would enhance the taste).
5. Pour a ladleful of batter on a heated dosa tawa. Let it cook on a medium flame for 2 minutes.
6. Turn it and let cook for 1 minute.
7. Serve hot with a chutney of your choice.

Tips

1. You could add finely chopped onions, coriander leaves and green chillies to the batter and then proceed to make the adai on the tawa.

Appam

(makes 10 appams)

Mrs. Rita Fernandez always had this on her Christmas menu at Bangalore. She shared this perfect recipe and it has always been a success.

Ingredients:

- 1 cup dosa rice soaked for 6 hours
- 1/3rd cup cooked rice
- 1/3rd cup grated coconut
- ½ tsp salt
- ½ tsp dried yeast
- 2 ½ tsp sugar
- Oil for making Appam

Method

1. Bloom the yeast in half a cup of lukewarm water and ½ tsp sugar for 10 minutes. It should turn bubbly and frothy. If it does not, then discard and start afresh.
2. Grind the rice, cooked rice and coconut in a mixie with a cup of water till fine and smooth. Add the salt and 2 tsp sugar and grind for a minute more. The batter should be thinner than a dosa batter and easy to pour.
3. Remove the flowing batter in a deep bowl.
4. Mix in the yeast.
5. Cover and keep it to ferment. 2 to 3 hours in a warm place would be enough. In a colder place, it may take longer.
6. The batter rises to almost 3 times.
7. Heat an appam chetty. Add 3 drops of oil and spread well.
8. Pour a ladle of the batter in the chetty and swirl it around. The edges should be thin and lacy and the centre thick. Cover and cook for 3 minutes till the edges start separating from the chetty.
9. Remove and serve with stew.

Idiappam

My friends Indu and Dr. Wajiha taught me this recipe. I make it in winter when the appams don't ferment well and have it for breakfast along with vegetable stew.

Ingredients

- 1 cup rice powder
- 1 tsp oil
- ¼ tsp salt
- 1 ½ cups water
- Oil for greasing

Method

1. Bring 1 ½ cups water to a boil. Add oil and salt to it.
2. Keeping it on a low flame, add the rice powder gradually and mix well till a dough is formed.
3. Put off the gas. Keep covered for 5 minutes.
4. While still warm, place the rice dough on a plate and knead well.
5. If the dough appears dry, you may add a little warm water and continue to make a smooth dough.
6. Grease the plates of an idli stand. Place 3 cups water in a cooker or steamer and bring to steam.
7. Make cylinders from the dough and place in a chakli press with the plates for sev.
8. Make idiappams by pressing on the dough till you get 3 inches round strings of idiappams.
9. Place in the idli moulds and steam for 8-10 minutes.
10. Cool slightly and remove. Serve with hot stew.

Tips

1. You could add ½ tsp of grated coconut while making the idiappams in between each layer. This is Dr. Wajiha's trick.

Vegetable Stew

This is a modified Indu's recipe which we have with Appam and Idiappam.

Ingredients:

- 1 medium carrot
- 10 french beans
- 1 medium potato
- 2 green chillies - slit
- 1 inch ginger cut in thin strips
- 10 curry leaves
- 1 onion chopped
- 1 packet (200ml) coconut milk
- 4 cloves
- 1 inch cinnamon
- Salt to taste

Method

1. Boil 2 cups water with the cloves and cinnamon.
2. Meanwhile chop the carrot, beans and potato into batons half inch long.
3. Add onion, carrot, beans, potato, green chilli, ginger and curry leaves to the boiling water.
4. Cook till the vegetables are done.
5. Add salt.
6. Reduce the flame and add the thick coconut milk.
7. (In case the mixture looks too watery, you made thicken it slightly with a tsp of rice powder mixed with water.)
8. Do not boil. Heat till it is about to boil.
9. Remove from heat.
10. **Optional:** Tadka with coconut oil and mustard seeds. (I don't give tadka)
11. Serve with appam and idiappam

Tomato Omelette

This would be on the menu of many south Indian hotels in Mumbai. A simple dish full of proteins and easy to make. It is also called Besan chilla.

Ingredients:

- 1 cup besan
- 1 small onion chopped finely
- 1 tomato chopped finely
- 1 green chilli chopped finely
- 1 tbsp finely chopped coriander
- ½ tsp salt or to taste
- ½ tsp chilli powder
- ½ tsp haldi
- Pinch of hing
- 1 tsp jeera
- Oil for tava frying

Method

1. Mix all above. Add water - around 1 cup to make it a flowing batter. Be sure that there are no lumps in the batter.
2. Heat the tava. Pour a ladle of batter. Put a tsp of oil if it is not a nonstick tava.
3. Cook on low to medium flame for 2 minutes. Flip it over. Cook for another 2 minutes.
4. Keep flipping and cooking till brown specks appear.
5. Serve hot with pudina or coconut chutney or tomato ketchup.

Tip

1. Sieving the besan before adding the rest of the ingredients avoids lumps.

Bhoplyache Gharge

(Makes 10)

A Maharashtrian sweet puri snack taught by my mother-in-law.

Ingredients

- 250 gm red pumpkin, grated. Approx. 2 cups
- 1 cup grated jaggery
- ¼ tsp salt
- 1 tsp ghee
- Atta for kneading
- Oil for frying

Method

1. Heat ghee in a kadhai. Add pumpkin. Sauté for 1 minute.
2. Add jaggery and cook till the fluid evaporates. Add salt.
3. Gradually add atta till you get a non- sticky dough- approximately 2 cups.
4. Cool in a plate.
5. Make 10 small balls. Roll into small puris and deep fry in medium hot oil.
6. Drain.
7. Serve hot with white butter and pickle.

Moong Dal Chillas

A protein packed breakfast delicacy. Easy to prepare.

Ingredients

- 1 cup whole moong dal soaked overnight
- 1 tbsp rice powder
- 1 green chilli chopped
- ½ inch ginger chopped
- 1 tbsp coriander leaves, chopped
- Salt to taste
- Oil for cooking

Method

1. Grind all the above ingredients except oil till you get a fine and smooth batter. The consistency should be that of a dosa batter.
2. Heat a dosa tawa. Prime with oil.
3. Spread one ladle of the batter on it.
4. Put half tsp oil on the sides. Cook for a minute on medium flame till the underside is light brown.
5. Turn the chilla and cook for 30 seconds.
6. Fold and serve hot.
7. You could stuff it with paneer burji or any other stuffing of your choice.
8. We eat it with mint chutney and cheese spread.

Tip

1. With the left over batter, I put chopped onions, coriander and chillies in it. And then cook it in an Appe pan and make pakodas (like paddu) or deep fry them as small pakodas.
2. The pakodas could be had by themselves with mint chutney or made into a chaat with beaten sweet curd, mint and imli chutney, chaat masala and bhuna jeera powder.

Vegetable Cutlet

(Makes 12)

My friend Usha Vidyashankar taught me this recipe for vegetable cutlet. This brought back many memories of my travels by the Deccan Queen from Mumbai to Pune where this was served.

Ingredients

- 1 big beetroot, 2 carrots, 1 small cabbage, all grated
- 3 medium potatoes boiled and mashed
- 1 medium onion chopped finely
- 3 bread slices freshly ground in a mixie
- 1 tbsp chopped coriander
- 2 green chillies, 1-inch ginger, 3 cloves garlic
- Salt to taste
- ½ tsp garam masala powder
- 2 tbsp oil
- 3 tbsp cornflour
- 3 tbsp bread crumbs/sooji/ powdered cornflakes
- Oil for deep frying

Method

1. Make a paste of ginger-garlic-green chilli. Heat 2 tbsp oil in a kadhai.
2. Add onions and sauté for 3 minutes. Add ginger-chili-garlic paste and fry for 2 minutes. Add beetroot, cabbage and carrot. Cover and cook till almost done.
3. Add potatoes and freshly ground bread. Mix well.
4. Add salt, garam masala and coriander leaves. Mix well. Adjust seasoning as per taste.
5. Allow the mixture to cool. Divide into 12 portions. Shape into cutlet roundels. Make a paste of cornflour in one cup water. Dip each cutlet into the paste and then roll in breadcrumbs or sooji or cornflakes powder.
6. Heat oil in a pan and fry the cutlets till golden brown.
7. Serve with sauce or in a burger.

Tip

1. For a crunchier covering repeat the cornflour crumb coating twice.

Bhel Puri

(to serve 4)

My eternal favorite from the streets of Mumbai.

Ingredients

- 2-3 cups murmura (puffed rice)
- 1 medium potato boiled and diced finely
- 1 medium onion chopped finely
- 2 tomatoes medium – deseeded and chopped finely
- 1 small raw mango (if available) – peeled and chopped finely
- 2 tbsp chopped coriander
- 1 green chilli chopped
- 4 tbsp tamarind chutney (see under chutneys)
- 2 tbsp mint chutney
- 8 papdis (store bought)
- 4 tbsp fine sev (store bought)

Method

1. Mix all above except the papdis and sev.
2. Mix 2 tbsp sev into the mixture. Keep the remaining for garnish.
3. Serve in individual portions with 2 papdis and sev as garnish

Tips

1. I like to serve it in canapes as a party snack.
2. In case the humidity has affected the puffed rice and it does not look crisp enough, put it in an oven tray. Bake at 60 degrees for 5 minutes and then use.

Chaats

The mint chutney and tamarind chutney are the ubiquitous requirements for chaats. The quantities can be adjusted as per your taste and spice levels. Chaat masala adds the extra zing.

Aloo chaat
Ingredients

- 4 medium potatoes – boiled, peeled and cut into 1 cm cubes
- Oil for deep/ shallow frying
- 2 tbsp mint chutney
- 2 tbsp tamarind chutney
- ½ tsp kala namak
- 1 tsp chaat masala

Method

1. Heat oil in a pan. You could either deep fry the diced boiled potatoes or shallow fry them till they just start turning brown.
2. Remove the potatoes from the oil. Place on a kitchen towel to drain the excess oil.
3. Keep aside till serving time.
4. Before serving, add both the chutneys, chaat masala and kala namak to the fried potatoes. Toss well. Serve immediately.

• • •

Sweet potato chaat

1. The ingredients and method are the same as for potato chaat. Substitute the potatoes with 2 medium size sweet potatoes.

• • •

Fruit chaat

1. 2 cups mixed chopped fruit (cut in 1 cm pieces) – including apples, bananas, pear, grapes (halved), pomegranate seeds, papaya, musk melon etc.

2. Mix all the fruits in a bowl. Add the juice of 1 lemon to prevent the fruits from darkening.
3. Mix in 1 ½ tbsp each of mint and tamarind chutney. Add 1 tsp chaat masala and half tsp kala namak. Toss. Serve chilled.

...

Bhalla papdi chaat (to serve 4)
Ingredients:

- 10 papdis (store bought)
- 3 Bhallas – soaked in water for 1 hour, drained, and cut roughly into pieces (see recipe for dahi vada)
- ½ cup kabuli channa (soaked overnight and boiled in the pressure cooker for 30 minutes with a little salt)
- Half cup boiled and diced potatoes
- 1 cup thick curd beaten with 1 tsp powdered sugar
- 2 tbsp mint chutney
- 2 tbsp tamarind chutney
- 1 tsp chaat masala
- ½ tsp red chilli powder
- ½ tsp roasted jeera powder

Method:

1. Arrange 3 papdis, 3-4 bhalla pieces, 1 tsp kabuli channa, and 1 tsp boiled potatoes on a plate.
2. Spoon 2 tbsp beaten curd on the above.
3. Top with mint and tamarind chutneys, chaat masala, jeera and red chilli powder.
4. Serve immediately.

Dahi Vada

(makes 15 vadas)

Mrs. Sharma senior, my neighbour at Delhi, always served the softest dahi Bhallas at Holi and told me that the trick to making soft, melt in the mouth dahi vadas, is the grinding. I use a grinder for the same. But this can also be done in a mixie. Just add little urad dal at a time with minimal water. Keep grinding and gradually add the rest of the dal in small batches. At the end, the ground paste should look shiny and glossy. Also, if using a mixie, then do beat before frying to get a light dahi vada.

Ingredients:
For vada

- 1 cup whole skinned urad dal
- ½ tsp salt
- Oil for deep frying

For dahi

- One litre thick curd
- 2 tbsp powdered sugar
- ½ tsp salt
- ½ tsp red chilli powder
- 1 tsp roasted jeera powder

Method:

1. Soak the urad dal for 2-3 hours. But no more than 3 hours. Grind in a grinder or mixie as mentioned above. Remove in a bowl, add salt and mix well.
2. Heat oil in a kadhai for deep frying. Once the oil is hot, reduce it to medium heat.
3. Make small flat balls of the batter in the palm of a wet hand. And gently slide into the oil carefully.
4. Or make the flat vadas on a clean plastic and slide into the oil. Or simply pour a spoonful of vada into the oil.
5. Fry on medium heat turning on both sides till golden brown in colour. Remove and drain on a kitchen towel.
6. Add the vadas to a big bowl of water and keep them soaked for 1-2 hours. The vadas will swell up and become soft.

For the dahi:

1. Beat the curd with sugar, salt, red chilli powder and jeera powder.
2. Press each vada to remove the excess water and soak it in the curd. Serve chilled with tamarind chutney.

Tip

1. The soaked vadas are used for bhalla papdi chaat.

Stuffed Garlic Bread

While on a visit to Chennai, I was invited by my friend Deepti Karmarkar for tea. She treated me with this yummy piping hot stuffed garlic bread and shared the following recipe with me.

Ingredients:
For bread

- 1 cup maida
- 1 tbsp oil
- ¼ tsp salt
- 1 tsp sugar
- 50 ml milk
- Dry yeast 1 tsp

For covering and stuffing

- 2 tbsp unsalted butter
- 3 cloves garlic, crushed
- ½ tsp salt
- ¼ tsp pepper powder
- ¼ tsp red chilli flakes.
- 2 tbsp each of red, yellow and green capsicum, chopped and sautéed in ½ tsp oil with a pinch of salt

Method

1. First activate the yeast. For this take milk. Heat it till lukewarm to touch along with the sugar. Mix in the dry yeast and keep it in a warm place for 10 minutes till bubbles start forming.
2. Add the milk with yeast to the maida, salt and oil. Knead well at least for 10 minutes till smooth. Cover with oil and keep aside for 2 hours until the dough doubles in size.
3. In the meanwhile, melt the butter. Add the garlic and sauté for 1 minute. Add salt, pepper and red chilli flakes. Keep aside. Preheat the oven for 10 minutes at 200 ℃.
4. Once the dough has risen, roll into a circle half cm thick and around 8 cm in diameter.

5. Brush the top of the dough with the melted butter mix. Spread the sautéed vegetables on one half. Add a tsp of the butter mixture on the vegetables.
6. Fold the other half so that you get a semi-circular shape. Brush the outsides of the dough with the butter. Rest for 15 minutes in a warm place, covered. Make slits on the upper half of the covering.
7. Bake for 20 minutes in a hot oven at 200℃. Slice and serve hot.

Tip

1. You could use a combination of vegetables for the stuffing. Capsicum, mushrooms are my favourites.
2. Addition of oregano or Italian spice mix and grated cheese to the vegetables also enhances the taste.

Pav Bhaji

A Saturday evening favorite at our house, and in summer, this is coupled with Mango Mastani for sumptuous meal. I feel that the best pav bhajis I've eaten are at Mumbai and no other city comes near it. The ladi pav which is available at Mumbai actually soaks up the delicious bhaji and makes you say "Yeh dil maange more".

Ingredients (serves 4)
For the Bhaji

- 3 potatoes boiled and mashed well
- 1 small cauliflower chopped into small pieces
- ½ medium carrot chopped into small pieces
- 1 small capsicum chopped finely
- ½ cup boiled green peas
- 1 medium onion chopped finely
- 3 tomatoes – 2 chopped and 1 pureed
- 4 cloves garlic
- 3 Kashmiri red chillies soaked in warm water for 15 minutes
- Salt to taste
- 2 tbsp Everest Pav Bhaji masala
- ½ tsp haldi
- 1 tsp Kashmiri red chilli powder
- 2 tsp oil
- 1 tbsp Amul butter
- For the Pav
- 10 ladi pavs
- 2 tsp Amul butter

Garnish

- 1 tbsp finely chopped coriander
- 1 wedge of nimbu
- ½ cup finely chopped onions
- Amul butter

Method

1. Steam the cauliflower and carrot for 6-8 minutes till soft. Mash them.
2. Drain the Kashmiri red chillies and make a paste along with the garlic.

3. Heat oil and butter in a pan. Sauté the onions till they are translucent. Add the capsicums and fry for 3 minutes.
4. Add the garlic-red chilli paste and fry for 1 minute.
5. Add the tomato pieces and puree and cook on medium flame till oil leaves the sides of the pan.
6. Add pav bhaji masala, haldi, Kashmiri red chilli powder and fry for 2 minutes.
7. Add the mashed potatoes, mashed vegetables and boiled peas. Mix well. Add salt.
8. The bhaji has a semi solid consistency. So add water to the above mixture and cook on a low flame for at least 10 minutes so that all the flavours soak in. Keep stirring intermittently and adjust the water and seasoning level.

Pav

1. Slit each pav in half. Apply butter liberally and toast it on a tava with the buttered side down. Once it is lightly cooked, repeat with the other side.
2. Place two pavs in a dish. Place the bhaji in a bowl with a dollop of butter on top.
3. Garnish with chopped onions, coriander leaves and a squeeze of nimbu.

Tip

1. Use Amul butter liberally to get the Mumbai pav bhaji feel. Sardar pav bhaji at Tardeo, Mumbai serves the most lip smacking generously buttered Pav bhaji.
2. I use Kashmiri red chillies and powder for the fiery red colour. You could use normal red chillies too.

Matki Patal Bhaji

My daughter Divya was given this family recipe by her mother-in-law Rajani Kamat. This was one of the most popular dishes at their family restaurant in Hubli.

Ingredients
Masala seasoning

- 1 tsp channa dal
- 1 tsp urad dal
- ¼ tsp white sesame seeds
- 3 cloves
- 1 inch cinnamon
- ½ tsp coriander seeds
- 1 tsp jeera
- 2 cloves garlic
- ½ cm ginger
- 4-6 methi seeds
- 10 curry leaves
- 2 tbsp grated fresh coconut
- 3 to 4 bydagi red chilli (as per spice tolerance)
- 2 tsp oil

Method

1. Heat oil in a pan. Add all the above ingredients and fry on low flame for 2-3 minutes. Grind with a little water to a fine paste.
2. For the masala seasoning if you are in a hurry you can replace this with store bought sambar powder added to roasted grated coconut

For the Matki

- 1 cup Matki (also called Moth). Soaked overnight, drained and left to sprout for a day.
- 1 potato finely chopped
- Salt to taste
- ½ tsp haldi

Method

1. Heat a pan. Add the above ingredients as mentioned under Matki and boil with 1 to 2 cups of water or enough water to completely submerge the sprouts. (This is called patal bhaji which means thin or runny in consistency). This should cook in about 12 to 15 minutes.

Tadka

- ½ tsp mustard seeds
- 6 curry leaves
- 1 medium onion chopped finely
- 1 tomato chopped finely
- 2 tsp oil
- 2 tsp jaggery

Method

1. Heat oil in a pan. Add the mustard seeds and fry till they crackle.
2. Add the curry leaves, onion, and fry till the onions are pink.
3. Add the tomatoes and cook till the tomatoes turn mushy.
4. Add the prepared masala paste to above and cook for 3 to 4 minutes.
5. Add the tadka to the boiling Matki and cook for 5 minutes.
6. Add 2 tsp of jaggery. This is a must to balance out the spice.
7. Serve hot garnished with chopped coriander leaves.
8. Serve with Puri or pav.

Kodubale

My friend Sushma Indrajit makes these crispy Kodubales especially during Diwali. Unsalted white butter adds to the taste and texture.

Ingredients

- 2 cups rice flour
- ½ cup maida
- ¼ cup grated coconut
- 2 green chillies
- ¼ tsp hing
- 1 tbsp chopped coriander leaves
- 3 tsp unsalted butter
- ½ tsp jeera
- Salt to taste
- Oil for frying

Method

1. Grind the coconut, green chillies, hing and coriander leaves to a fine powder without water.
2. Add the rest of the ingredients and the ground powder to the rice flour and maida.
3. Mix well and then add water gradually to knead to a stiff dough.
4. Make small marble size balls from the dough and roll each ball with between greased palms to make a cylinder with tapered ends.
5. Join the ends together to make rings.
6. Meanwhile heat oil in a frying pan and keep at medium heat.
7. Fry the rings till they turn brown.
8. Cool and store in an airtight container.

Poha Chiwda

A typical Maharashtrian Chiwda which I make during Diwali. I use thin poha (flattened rice) for this as opposed to the thick poha used to make the breakfast dish.

Ingredients

- 250 gm thin poha sieved to remove the powder
- 3 tbsp groundnuts
- 3 tbsp cashewnuts, halved
- 3 tbsp kismis
- 2 tbsp thinly sliced copra (dry coconut)
- 2 tbsp roasted channa dal
- 4 green chillies chopped into half cm
- 20 curry leaves
- 1 tsp white til
- ½ tsp haldi
- ½ tsp salt (or to taste)
- 1 ½ tsp powdered sugar
- ½ tsp mustard seeds
- ½ tsp jeera
- ¼ tsp hing
- 3 tbsp oil

Method

1. Heat a thick bottomed kadhai. Keep at low heat, roast the poha till it is crisp and crackles when pressed between the fingers. The poha shrinks a bit at this stage and may curl up. Do this in batches so that it crisps uniformly. Keep aside in a large pan.
2. Heat the oil in the same kadhai.
3. Keeping the flame low medium, first fry the copra slices till they just start turning brown. This happens very quickly or else it burns. Drain and remove on a plate.
4. Then fry the groundnuts, cashews, kismis and roasted channa dal separately in the same oil. Drain and remove on a plate.
5. Add mustard seeds to the oil and fry till they crackle. Add jeera and til and fry for one minute.
6. Add the green chillies and curry leaves and fry till both are crisp.
7. Add haldi and hing. Fry for 30 seconds.

8. Keeping the flame at low, add the poha and fried groundnuts, copra, cashews, kismis and channa dal.
9. Add the salt and sugar. Mix well turning it repeatedly till the whole mixture is pale yellow in colour.
10. Put off the gas. Let the mixture cool. Store in airtight containers.

• • •

Cornflakes Chiwda

Eating cornflakes daily for breakfast becomes boring. This chiwda is a good way to consume cornflakes as an evening snack.

1. The method and ingredients are the same as for poha chiwda. Except replace the poha with 3 cups of cornflakes. Lightly roast the cornflakes in a kadhai with 1 tsp oil for 2-3 minutes and remove. The rest of the procedure remains the same.

• • •

Murmura Chiwda

A light snack to be had with evening tea.

Ingredients

- 2 cups murmura (puffed rice)
- 10 curry leaves
- 2 tbsp groundnuts
- ½ tsp red chilli powder
- ½ tsp haldi
- ½ tsp mustard seeds
- Pinch of hing
- Salt to taste
- 1 tsp oil

Method

1. Roast and keep aside the murmura in a pan.
2. Heat the oil. Keeping it on low flame, fry the groundnuts. Drain and keep the groundnuts aside.
3. Add the mustard seeds and let it crackle. Add haldi, hing and curry leaves.
4. Fry till the curry leaves crisps up.
5. Add the murmura, groundnuts, red chilli powder and salt and toss well on low flame for 2-3 minutes. Cool.
6. Store in an airtight container.

Main course

- Avial
- Vegetable Sagu
- Cabbage Poriyal
- Peeth Perun Capsicum
- Corn Capsicum Bhaji
- Baingan Bharta
- Cheese Baingan
- Exotic Cauliflower
- Lychee Kofta
- Navratan Korma
- Paneer Bhurji
- Sarson Ka Saag
- Saucy Paneer
- Vegetarian Shepherd's Pie
- Stuffed Bhindi
- Bhindi Do Pyaaza
- Asian Stir Fried Vegetables

Avial

This dish brings back memories of my mother's festival menu. The more sour the curd, the tastier the dish is. It is to be had with rice.

Ingredients

- 100 gm red pumpkin cut into half inch cubes
- 100 gm white pumpkin cut into half inch cubes
- 1 drumstick cut into 1 inch long pieces
- 1 carrot cut into half inch pieces
- 1 potato cut into half inch pieces
- 2 green chillies
- 1 tsp jeera
- Half cup grated coconut
- 1 cup curd
- 8-10 curry leaves
- ½ tsp salt
- ½ tsp haldi
- 1 tsp oil
- ½ tsp mustard seeds

Method

1. Boil the above vegetables in 1 and ½ cups water till done. Drain the excess water.
2. Grind the grated coconut, green chillies and jeera into a fine paste with little water.
3. Add boiled vegetables, paste, haldi and salt with half a cup of water in a pan.
4. Cook for 2 to 3 minutes on medium flame.
5. Whisk the curd and add to above.
6. Cook continuously on a high flame till it just starts to boil.
7. Remove from the gas.
8. Heat oil in a tempering vessel. Add mustard seeds and fry till they crackle. Put off the flame and add the curry leaves. Pour the tempering on the avial gravy and mix well.
9. Serve hot with rice.

Vegetable Sagu

This is my aunt Vasantha Raju's special sagu which she used to serve with hot puris. She had magic in her hands and could whip up delicacies in a jiffy till her last days.

Ingredients

- 1 cup chopped mixed vegetables (carrot, beans, cauliflower). The vegetables have to be half cm cubes
- 1 potato chopped into ½ cm pieces
- ½ cup green peas
- ½ tsp salt or to taste
- ½ tsp mustard seeds
- ½ tsp urad dal
- 1 tsp oil

To grind

- ½ cup grated coconut
- 1 ½ tbsp chutney dal
- 2 green chillies
- 2 tbsp chopped coriander leaves
- ½ inch ginger chopped
- 1 tsp jeera
- Grind the above with water to make a smooth paste.

Method

1. Boil vegetables in 2 cups water till just done. Drain and keep aside
2. Heat the oil in a pan. Add mustard seeds. Once they splutter add the urad dal and fry till light brown.
3. Add the vegetables, ground paste, salt, and 2 cups water.
4. Stir on a low flame till the mixture thickens.
5. Serve hot with puri or rava idli.

Cabbage Poriyal

A simple, light, dry vegetable dish from South India. This is had with rice and rasam.

Ingredients

- 1 medium cabbage
- 2 green chillies
- ½ cup grated coconut
- 1 tbsp coriander leaves chopped
- 10 curry leaves
- ½ tsp haldi
- Salt to taste
- 1 tsp urad dal
- ½ tsp mustard seeds
- Pinch of hing
- 2 tsp oil

Method

1. Chop the cabbage finely. Rinse well.
2. Grind the coconut with the chillies, without water. Keep aside
3. Heat oil in a pan. Add mustard seeds and fry till they splutter. Add the urad dal and fry for 1 minute on low flame. Add curry leaves, hing and haldi.
4. Add the chopped cabbage and salt. Mix well.
5. Cook covered on low flame stirring intermittently.
6. Add a little water if the mixture appears dry.
7. The cabbage will take around 10-12 minutes to cook and become soft.
8. Then add the ground coconut-chilli mixture. Stir well and cook for another 2 minutes.
9. Serve hot garnished with coriander leaves.

Tips

My friend Dr. Wajiha adds a tablespoon of sprouted moong while cooking the cabbage to give an additional crunch.

• • •

Beetroot Poriyal

1. The method is the same as for cabbage poriyal. Instead of cabbage, use 2 beetroots which have been peeled and then grated or chopped finely. The rest of the procedure is the same.

• • •

Beans Poriyal

1. The method is the same as for cabbage poriyal. Instead of cabbage, use 250 gm of French beans which have been chopped into fine pieces. The rest of the procedure is the same. Add half a cup of water while cooking the beans and check intermittently if it appears dry.

• • •

Carrot and Beans Poriyal

1. The method is the same as for cabbage poriyal. Instead of cabbage, use 150 gm of French beans and 2 finely chopped peeled carrots. The rest of the procedure is the same. Add half a cup of water while cooking the beans and carrot and check intermittently if it appears dry.

• • •

Chow Chow Poriyal

Chow Chow is a summer squash available in South India. It has a slightly sweet taste.

1. Peel and chop 2 chow chows into 1 cm cubes.
2. The method is the same as for cabbage poriyal.
3. Add half a cup of water while cooking the chow chow and check intermittently if it appears dry.

Peeth Perun Capsicum

This is a Maharashtrian dry vegetable. It is had with aamti (Maharashtrian arhar dal) and rice or roti.

Ingredients

- 3 capsicums chopped into half cm pieces
- 1 onion chopped (optional)
- 3 tbsp besan
- ½ tsp jeera
- ½ tsp mustard seeds
- Salt to taste
- ½ tsp chilli powder
- 2 tsp coriander powder
- ½ tsp haldi
- Pinch of hing
- 8-10 curry leaves
- 3 tbsp oil
- 1 tbsp chopped coriander leaves

Method

1. Heat a kadhai. Roast the besan till the raw smell goes off and it turns light brown. This takes approx. 5-7 minutes on low flame. Remove the besan in a plate.
2. In the same kadhai, heat oil. Add mustard seeds and jeera and fry for 1 minute till the mustard crackles.
3. Add hing, haldi and curry leaves. Stir for half minute.
4. Add the chopped onions and sauté till light pink.
5. Add chopped capsicums. Cook in an open pan till capsicums are almost done.
6. Add salt, red chilli powder and coriander powder. Mix well.
7. Add besan slowly, mixing well.
8. Then sprinkle 2 tbsp water, 1 tbsp at a time and mix. The mixture should not appear dry.
9. Serve hot garnished with coriander leaves.

Corn Capsicum Sabji

I usually make this simple dish during the monsoons, when fresh sweet corn is available in plenty. I do not use frozen corn for this.

Ingredients:

- 2 medium capsicums, diced into half cm pieces
- 1 medium fresh corn
- 1 medium onion chopped
- ½ tsp freshly ground pepper
- ½ tsp salt or to taste
- 2 tsp oil

Method:

1. Boil the corn in water for 8 to 10 minutes, covered.
2. With a knife, take out the kernels.
3. Heat the oil in a pan.
4. Fry the onions till just done.
5. Add the capsicum and stir fry for 2-3 minutes.
6. Add the corn kernels and cook for 2 minutes.
7. Add pepper and salt.
8. Serve hot with rotis.

Baingan Bharta

(Serves 2)

A simple dish with the smoky flavour of baingans. Some folks add 1 tbsp of boiled green peas to the baingan. I believe that the good amount of tomatoes provides the necessary tanginess to the otherwise bland vegetable.

Ingredients

- 1 medium brinjal - the one used for bharta
- 1 onion chopped
- 2 large tomatoes chopped
- 1 green chilli chopped
- Salt to taste
- 2 tbsp oil
- 1 tbsp coriander leaves chopped

Method

1. Roast the brinjal over the gas flame till the skin is charred. Cool and peel the skin. Chop the cooked brinjal pulp.
2. Heat oil in a frying pan.
3. Add the onions and chilli. Sauté till the onions turn golden at the edges.
4. Add the tomatoes and cook till the tomatoes are pulpy.
5. Add the brinjal pulp and cook on medium flame for 3-4 minutes.
6. Add salt and mix.
7. Garnish with coriander leaves.
8. Serve hot with roti or paratha.

Cheese Baingan

This is one dish I always make at every party and I consider it my signature dish. I have had many brinjal hating friends convert to brinjal likers, after eating this. It is easy to make, can be prepared and assembled in advance and just popped into the oven at the time of serving.

Ingredients

- 2 large brinjals (the bharta variety)
- 2 tsp salt
- 3 tbsp tomato ketchup (any brand)
- 5 cloves of garlic, crushed
- 1 tsp freshly ground pepper
- Oil for deep frying
- 3-4 tbsp grated processed cheese (I use only Amul cheese)

Method

1. Dice the brinjals into half inch pieces. Place the brinjal pieces in a vessel and salt the pieces well. This helps in sweating the brinjal and makes it slightly soft.
2. Keep the salted brinjals aside for 15 to 20 minutes.
3. Heat the oil in a kadhai. Bring it to medium heat.
4. Take a handful of the salted brinjals, wash under water. Squeeze gently.
5. Fry the brinjals in the oil till brown.
6. Drain on a kitchen towel.
7. Keep doing this in batches till all the brinjal pieces are fried and drained.
8. Place the pieces in an oven proof serving bowl.
9. Mix in the tomato ketchup, crushed garlic and pepper powder well, such that each piece of the brinjal is coated.
10. Cover the brinjal mixture with grated cheese.
11. At the time of serving, heat it in a microwave for 3-4 minutes till the cheese melts.

Exotic Cauliflower

While at Bangalore, my laboratory friends would occasionally indulge in the buffet at a nearby hotel – Manthan. And they used to serve this exotic cauliflower gravy. After savouring it and guessing the ingredients, I tried this at home and it did come out almost like the hotel one.

Ingredients

- 1 medium cauliflower, cut into florets
- 3 onions cut in quarters
- 1 tsp ginger garlic paste
- ½ cup curd, beaten
- 2 tbsp cashews, soaked for half an hour
- ¾ tsp salt or to taste
- ½ tsp pepper powder
- 3 tbsp oil
- Whole spices- 1 tej patta, 4 cloves, 1 inch cinnamon
- ½ tsp green cardamom powder
- 2 tbsp fresh cream

Method

1. Blanch the cauliflower florets in boiling water for 2 minutes. Remove and drain.
2. Boil the onions for 8-10 minutes in a pan with 1 cup water. Drain and puree in a mixie.
3. Grind the soaked cashews to a fine paste.
4. Heat oil in a pan. Shallow fry the blanched cauliflower till brown specks appear. Remove and drain on a kitchen towel. In the remaining oil, put the whole spices and lightly fry for 1 minute on a medium flame.
5. Add the boiled onion paste and sauté till done and oil starts leaving the sides of the pan. Add the ginger - garlic paste and fry for one minute. Add curd and cook on high flame for 2 minutes.
6. Reduce the flame and add the cashew paste. Stirring continuously, cook for 3 minutes.
7. Add the cauliflower, cardamom powder and salt. Add water to make a thick gravy.
8. Check salt and the consistency of the gravy.
9. Cook for 5 minutes on a low flame.
10. Add beaten cream just before serving.

Lychee Kofta in Makhani gravy

This summer, the Kolkata markets were flooded with luscious lychees. Many years ago, I had ordered stuffed lychees at a restaurant in Girgaum, Mumbai and thought I'd try out this recipe. It worked out well.

Ingredients
For Koftas

- 12 lychees
- Fresh paneer from half litre milk
- ¼ tsp pepper powder
- ¼ tsp salt
- 1 tsp chopped coriander

For Makhani gravy

- 6 ripe tomatoes chopped roughly
- 1 medium onion chopped roughly
- 3 cloves garlic chopped
- 1 inch ginger chopped
- 8 to 10 cashews
- 3 cloves
- 1 inch cinnamon
- 3 green cardamoms
- 1 black cardamom
- 2 bay leaves
- 1 tsp Kashmiri red chilli powder
- Half tsp salt
- Pinch of sugar (if tomatoes are sour)
- 1 and ½ tsp kasoori methi crushed
- 1 tbsp butter
- 2 tbsp cream (optional)

Method
Koftas:

1. Peel the lychees. Make a slit and remove the seed. Keep aside.

2. Mash the paneer with salt, coriander leaves and pepper powder. You could add chopped nuts too.
3. Make small balls. Stuff into the lychees. And keep aside till serving time.

Makhani gravy:

1. Boil 3 cups water along with the tomatoes, onion, ginger, garlic, cashews and whole spices as mentioned above. Cover. Keep on medium heat and boil for 25 minutes.
2. Let it cool. Remove the cinnamon, bay leaves, black cardamom.
3. Puree the above and strain it.
4. Heat the butter in a pan. Add the above tomato puree, Kashmiri red chilli powder, salt. Crush kasoori methi and add to above.
5. Cook for 5 minutes.
6. Before serving, add the lychee koftas, cover and cook for 3 minutes.
7. Garnish with beaten cream and serve hot.

Navratan Korma

A lightly spiced delicacy consisting of vegetables in a white gravy.

Ingredients

- 1 cup mixed vegetables diced – beans, carrot, potato
- ½ cup fresh peas, boiled
- 3 onions cut in quarters
- 1 tsp ginger garlic paste
- 1 green chilli chopped
- ½ cup curd, beaten
- 2 tbsp cashews, soaked for half an hour
- 1 tbsp cashews - halved and fried
- 50 gm paneer diced into 1 cm cubes
- 2 slices tinned pineapple chopped into 1 cm pieces (optional)
- ½ tsp salt or to taste
- 1 tbsp oil
- 1 tbsp ghee
- Whole spices- 1 tej patta, 4 cloves, 1 inch cinnamon, 4 green elaichi

Method

1. Steam the vegetables for 5 minutes.
2. Boil the onions for 8-10 minutes in a pan with 1 cup water. Drain and puree in a mixie.
3. Grind the soaked cashews to a fine paste.
4. Heat oil and ghee in a pan. Put the whole spices and lightly fry for 1 minute on a medium flame.
5. Add the boiled onion paste and sauté till done and oil starts leaving the sides of the pan. Add the ginger-garlic paste and fry for one minute. Add curd and cook on high flame for 2 minutes.
6. Reduce the flame and add the cashew paste. Stirring continuously, cook for 3 minutes.
7. Add the steamed vegetables, boiled peas, paneer and pineapple (optional). Add salt. Add water to make a thick gravy. Cook for 5 minutes on a low flame. Serve hot garnished with fried cashews.
8. For a richer taste, garnish with beaten cream before serving.

Paneer Bhurji

This dish is made when I am lazy and want to whip up something quick to go with parathas in the snack box or dinner.

Ingredients

- 200 gm paneer – crumbled
- 1 medium onion chopped
- 1 medium capsicum chopped
- 1 medium tomato chopped
- Salt to taste
- ½ tsp freshly ground pepper
- 2 tsp oil
- ¼ tsp haldi

Method

1. Heat the oil in a pan. Keeping on medium heat, fry the onions till translucent.
2. Add haldi and the capsicum and fry for 2 minutes.
3. Add the tomatoes and cook till tomatoes are soft.
4. Add the crumbled paneer, salt and pepper and sauté for 2-3 minutes.
5. Do not overcook or else the paneer will become tough.
6. Serve hot, rolled into a paratha.

Tip

1. If you have some left over red and yellow capsicums in the refrigerator, these can also be chopped and added to give a colorful bhurji.

Sarson ka Saag

My friend's Dr. Mandeep Kang's mother Mrs. Ginderjeet Kaur Kang invited me for lunch at Chandigarh. That was the first time I really enjoyed eating this with delicious makki ki roti and a dollop of white unsalted butter and crushed jaggery. This is a variation of many recipes that I learnt from friends while at Delhi. Since I can't make makki ki roti, we have it with parathas at home.

Ingredients

- Half kg mustard leaves (sarson saag)
- 250 gm palak
- 250 gm bathua
- 50 gm methi leaves
- ½ inch ginger chopped
- ½ inch ginger grated
- 6 cloves garlic chopped
- 2 green chillis chopped
- 1 onion chopped fine
- 1 tomato chopped fine
- Maize flour 2 tsp (or substitute with besan)
- Hing a pinch
- Salt to taste
- 3 tsp ghee

Method

1. Clean and wash the greens - leaves only. Take the tender stalks of sarson and finely chop. Discard the thick stalks.
2. Put the greens, 1 green chilli, chopped ginger in the pressure cooker with half a cup of water. Close the lid and cook for 20 minutes after the whistle.
3. Open the cooker. Add the maize flour and let cool. Mash coarsely either in the mixie or with a potato masher.
4. Heat ghee in a kadhai. Add hing. Add garlic and fry for half a minute.
5. Add onion, grated ginger and 1 chopped green chilli. Fry till the onion is light brown.
6. Add the tomatoes and cook till the tomatoes are done.
7. Add the mashed greens, salt and simmer for 5 minutes.
8. Serve hot with makki ki roti and grated jaggery and white butter on the side.

Saucy Paneer

A simple paneer dish which the children love. And can be made in 15 minutes.

Ingredients

- 200 gm paneer cut into half inch squares
- 2 medium tomatoes
- 1 medium onion
- 1 medium green capsicum
- ½ tsp pepper powder
- ½ tsp salt
- 1 tsp soya sauce
- 3 tbsp tomato sauce
- 2 tsp oil

Method

1. Chop all vegetables into half inch squares.
2. Heat the oil in a pan.
3. Add the onions and fry till pale pink on a medium heat.
4. Add capsicum and sauté for 1 minute.
5. Add tomatoes. Cook till vegetables are almost done.
6. Add the sauces, pepper and salt. Mix well.
7. Add half a cup of water. Bring to boil. Add paneer. Cook for 3 to 4 minutes till paneer is soft.
8. Serve hot with roti or paratha.

Vegetarian Shepherd's Pie

My friend Dr. Debmita gave me this recipe. This is such a filling wholesome dish and can be had with garlic bread and a bowl of soup.

Ingredients
For the base

- 1 cup whole masoor dal soaked for 3-4 hours
- 4 cloves garlic chopped
- 1 medium onion chopped
- 100 gm paneer chopped into 1 cm squares
- 100 gm mushrooms chopped and sautéed in oil (optional)
- 100 gm carrots chopped and steamed for 5 minutes (optional)
- 2 tsp soya sauce
- ½ tsp freshly ground pepper
- Salt to taste

Method

1. Drain the soaked dal. Boil the masoor dal in the pressure cooker with the garlic, onions and salt till done. This should take 10-12 minutes.
2. Heat a pan. Add the cooked masoor dal in it. Add pepper powder, soya sauce and paneer.
3. Cook until the mixture is quite dry. Place this mixture on the base of an oven proof dish.

For the potato topping

- 5 potatoes
- 4 tbsp butter
- ½ cup milk
- Salt to taste
- ½ tsp pepper powder

Method

1. Wash and peel the potatoes. Chop into quarters and place in boiling water. Boil in a partially closed pan till the potatoes are fork done. This would take 15-20 minutes.
2. Drain and place in a pan. Mash with a fork. While still hot, put the butter, salt, pepper and half the milk on the potatoes.
3. Whisk or mash well till you get a creamy texture. You may add more milk if necessary.
4. Preheat the oven to 180°C for 10 minutes. Spoon the potato mash over the lentil base and spread evenly. Bake at 180°C for 10-15 minutes till the top of the potatoes is brown. Serve hot.

Stuffed Bhindi

Bhindi is the favorite vegetable at our house. My husband could have it at all meals without getting bored. So I do try and make different preparations of this vegetable.

Ingredients

- 250 gm bhindi, preferably medium in size
- 2 small onions
- 3 tbsp oil
- Salt to taste
- 2 tbsp coriander powder
- 1 tsp jeera powder
- 1 tbsp amchur
- ½ tsp red chilli powder
- ½ tsp haldi
- ½ tsp garam masala powder
- ½ tsp chaat masala

Method

1. Wash and dry the bhindi well. Cut the top and bottom end. Make a slit on one side of the bhindis.
2. Peel the onions and quarter it, not through and through. It should resemble a flower.
3. Mix all the dry powders mentioned above. Stuff the bhindis with a little masala mix. Also stuff the onions with the same.
4. Heat the oil in a thick bottomed frying pan.
5. Keeping on low flame, add the stuffed bhindis and onions. Cover and cook for 10 minutes, stirring intermittently.
6. Check if the bhindis are fully cooked and serve with rotis.

Tips

1. The bhindis have to be completely pat dried before chopping or else is becomes slimy.
2. If the bhindis have been taken out of the refrigerator, they must be brought to room temperature before cutting.

Bhindi Do Pyaaza

This bhindi dish with a little gravy is delightful. Have it hot with rotis.

Ingredients

- 250 gm bhindi
- 2 medium onions sliced
- 2 tomatoes grated
- ½ inch ginger grated
- 1 green chilli chopped
- 2 tsp besan
- ½ tsp haldi
- Salt to taste
- ½ tsp red chilli powder
- ½ tsp garam masala
- 1 tbsp coriander powder
- ½ tsp jeera
- 2 tbsp oil
- Oil for frying the bhindi
- ½ cup milk

Method

1. Wash and pat dry the bhindi. Chop into 1 inch pieces. Make a paste of the ginger and green chilli.
2. Heat the oil in a pan. Keeping the heat medium, deep fry the bhindi for 2-3 minutes, till it just starts turning brown. Remove on a kitchen towel.
3. Heat 2 tbsp oil in a pan, add jeera, haldi and fry for a minute.
4. Add the onions and fry till translucent. Add the ginger-chilli paste. Fry for 2 minutes.
5. Add tomatoes and cook till oil leaves the sides of the pan. Add red chilli powder and coriander powder. Add besan and fry on a low heat for 2 minutes.
6. Add milk and ½ cup water. Boil well and bring it on simmer.
7. Add the bhindis, salt and garam masala. Cook on low flame for 3-4 minutes. Serve hot

Asian Stir Fried Vegetables

My son in law Dr. Ritweez Sahu is a food aficionado. He loves different cuisines and also likes cooking. This is one his creations to be had as a side with noodles.

Ingredients

- 1 carrot – peeled and cut diagonally into 2 mm ovals
- 10 French beans, stringed and cut into 1 inch pieces
- 100 gm paneer or tofu cubed into 1 cm pieces
- 1 tbsp peanuts
- 2 tsp cornflour
- 2 red chillies
- 1 tbsp ginger-garlic minced
- 1 tbsp soy sauce
- 1 tbsp honey
- ¼ tsp red chilli flakes
- Salt to taste
- ½ tsp white sesame seeds, toasted
- 4-5 drops of sesame oil
- ¼ tsp Ajinomoto (optional)
- 4 tsp oil

Method

1. Marinate the paneer/tofu cubes in salt, chilli flakes, 1 tsp soya sauce and cornflour for 20-30 minutes.
2. Heat a pan with 1 tsp oil. Lightly cook the marinated paneer in it till light brown.
3. Mix the remaining soya sauce, sesame seeds, honey, sesame oil and salt.
4. Heat a kadai with 3 tsp oil. Fry the peanuts on medium flame till brown. Remove and keep aside.
5. To the same oil, fry the red chillies for a minute. Then add ginger-garlic mince and fry on low flame for 2-3 minutes. Add the carrots and beans and fry on low flame till they are cooked but still are crunchy. Add the prepared soya sauce mixture. Add the paneer and peanuts.
6. Mix well and cook on low flame for 2-3 minutes. Serve hot.

Dals and Liquid accompaniments

- Aamti
- Tomato Saar
- Cholar Dal
- Maa Chole di Dal
- Sookhi Urad Dal
- Tomato Rasam
- Sambar
- Mor Kuzhambu
- Kabuli Chana
- Sinful Punjabi Chole
- Dalma

Aamti

A staple in every Maharashtrian kitchen. This was one of the earliest recipes taught by my mother-in-law and is prepared almost three times a week at home.

Ingredients

- 1 cup arhar dal
- 1 tomato finely chopped
- 2 green chillies slit
- 6-8 curry leaves
- 2 tbsp finely chopped coriander leaves
- 1 tbsp ghee
- ½ tsp jeera
- ½ tsp mustard seeds
- Hing – a pinch
- ½ tsp haldi powder
- ½ tsp salt or to taste
- 1 tsp sugar

Method

1. Boil the dal in a pressure cooker with haldi and salt for 10 minutes after the whistle.
2. Mash the dal well with a potato masher.
3. Heat ghee in a pan.
4. Once it is hot, add jeera and mustard seeds. Fry for a minute till the mustard seeds crackle.
5. Add the green chillies and curry leaves. Fry for half a minute. Add hing.
6. Then add the chopped tomatoes. Cook on medium heat till the tomatoes turn soft.
7. Add the mashed dal and sugar. Add water to adjust the consistency to a thick pouring liquid.
8. Bring to a boil. Reduce the heat and simmer for 5-6 minutes. Check for salt seasoning.
9. Garnish with coriander leaves.
10. Serve hot.

Tomato Saar

A Maharashtrian delicacy. Ideal for a wintry evening

Ingredients (Serves 2)

- 4 medium sized tomatoes, preferably red ones
- 1 green chilli
- ½ tsp salt or to taste
- 2 tsp sugar
- ¾ cup (150 ml) curd
- 1 tsp ghee
- ½ tsp jeera
- 1 tbsp chopped coriander leaves

Method:

1. Chop the tomatoes and grind in a mixie with the chilli.
2. When almost done add the curd and grind till smooth.
3. Pass it through a sieve, discard the coarse residue present in the sieve.
4. Place the puree in a heavy bottom vessel on the gas. Add water till it is of a pouring consistency.
5. Add salt and sugar and keep stirring on moderate heat for 4-5 minutes. Do not let it boil.
6. Adjust the salt and sugar according to taste.
7. Put off the gas.
8. Add coriander leaves.
9. Heat 1 tsp ghee in a tadka pan. Once hot, add jeera and put off gas. Pour this into the Saar.
10. This can be had as a soup or with rice.

Tips

1. You can use 1 cup coconut milk instead of curd. Rest of the procedure remains the same.
2. You may add more of less sugar depending upon the tartness of the tomatoes.

Cholar Dal

My Bengali friends Smeeta and Dr. Chandreyee have their own spins on this favorite dal of mine. I've put together this recipe with my tweaks. I enjoy the sweet and salty taste with the hint of spices.

Ingredients

- 1 cup chana dal soaked for 2-3 hours
- 2 green chillies slit
- Half inch ginger grated
- 1 inch cinnamon stick
- 1 bay leaf
- 3 cloves
- 3 green elaichi
- ½ tsp haldi
- ½ tsp salt or to taste
- 1 tsp jaggery crushed
- 1 tsp oil

Method

1. Heat the oil in a cooker.
2. Add the cloves, cinnamon, bay leaf and elaichi. Stir for one minute.
3. Add the ginger and green chillies. Stir.
4. Drain the chana dal and add it to above. Add the rest of the ingredients.
5. Stir for one minute.
6. Add 3 cups of water. Close the cooker and cook for 12 minutes after the whistle.
7. Check the seasonings. Adjust the consistency if it is too watery by boiling in an open pan.
8. Serve hot.

Tips:

1. For an authentic cholar dal, fry some thinly sliced dry coconut (copra) and add to the dal.

Maa Chole di Dal

My friend Dr. Anupama Devgan served this dal for dinner. It was simply so delicious that we kept having bowlfuls of these. Now it is a regular staple at my house.

Ingredients:

- ½ cup chana dal
- ½ cup chilka urad dal (split)
- 2 inch piece ginger (grind 1 inch with the chilli, finely chop 1 inch)
- 2 green chillies
- 1 tsp salt or to taste
- ½ tsp haldi
- 3 tbsp ghee
- 1 onion finely chopped
- 2 tomatoes grated
- 2 tsp dhania power
- 1 tsp Kashmiri chilli powder
- ½ tsp garam masala
- 3 tbsp chopped coriander leaves

Method:

1. Soak the chana dal and urad chilka in water for 2 to 3 hours.
2. Cook in a pressure cooker along with freshly ground ginger + green chilli (about an inch of ginger and two green chillies) paste, salt and haldi. Add water to 1 cm above the dals.
3. Also add grated tomatoes in the cooker.
4. Cook for 15 minutes after the whistle.
5. For the tadka - Heat the ghee. Fry onions, chopped ginger, dhania powder, Kashmiri red chilli powder and garam masala.
6. Add the above tadka to the cooked dal and simmer for 5 minutes.
7. Garnish with fresh coriander.

Tips:

1. What is must for the dal is plenty of ginger and desi ghee! So be generous.

Sookhi Urad Dal

Mrs. Poonam Sandhu introduced me to this dal in Bangalore, and it has become a family favorite especially when a vegetable with gravy is made as a side.

Ingredients

- 1 cup urad dal dhuli (without skin)
- 2 inch ginger grated
- 2 tomatoes chopped fine
- 1 onion, 1 green chilli finely chopped
- Hing – a pinch
- ½ tsp jeera
- ½ tsp salt
- ½ tsp red chilli powder
- ½ tsp garam masala powder
- ½ tsp amchur powder
- 1 tbsp chopped coriander leaves

Method

1. Wash and soak the urad dal for half an hour. Drain.
2. Boil 5 cups of water. Add half the grated ginger and haldi. Add the urad dal. Cook on a medium flame, uncovered. Check the dal periodically crushing between fingers till it is almost done. This will take around half an hour. DO NOT pressure cook the dal. Drain the dal when done.
3. Heat oil in a pan. Add jeera, hing and fry for a minute.
4. Add onion and fry till translucent. Add the ginger and green chilli. Fry for half a minute.
5. Add the chopped tomatoes and cook till the tomatoes are done. Add the drained urad dal, red chilli powder, salt, garam masala powder and amchur. Mix well.
6. Cook on low flame for 2-3 minutes. Check salt and seasoning.
7. Remove from flame. Serve hot garnished with coriander leaves.

Tips:

1. Do not boil the urad dal in the pressure cooker; if overdone it turns slimy.
2. What we need is cooked dal just done with separate grains.

Tomato Rasam

Rasam and rice is my soul food. I have it when I'm happy or sick or bored with routine food or simply have the rasam as soup on a wintry evening. This is my mother's recipe. She used to make her own rasam powder, but I always use MTR Rasam powder.

Ingredients (Serves 4)

- 1 tbsp arhar dal
- 1 small ball of tamarind
- 1 tomato finely chopped
- 5-6 curry leaves
- 1 tbsp coriander leaves chopped
- 1 tsp ghee
- ½ tsp mustard seeds
- ¼ tsp haldi
- Pinch of sugar
- 1 tbsp MTR Rasam powder

Method

1. Soak the dal in water for half an hour. Boil with haldi and salt in a pressure cooker for 10 minutes. Once done, mash the dal till smooth.
2. Soak the tamarind in quarter cup water for 15 minutes. Strain the puree and liquid, discard the residue.
3. Boil 2 cups water along with the chopped tomato. Add the tamarind liquid.
4. Boil till the raw smell of tamarind disappears.
5. Add rasam powder, boiled and mashed dal, and sugar. Simmer for 4 minutes. Adjust salt.
6. Add chopped coriander leaves.

For Tempering

1. Heat ghee in a pan. Add mustard seeds and fry till they crackle and then add curry leaves.
2. Serve hot in winters as a soup or with steamed rice.

Sambar

My friend Dr. Neelamani gave me this recipe and then onwards I use store bought sambar powder very sparingly. I usually make this sambar with small pearl onions and serve it piping hot with soft idlis.

Ingredients
For the sambar masala

- 1 tsp oil
- 3 tbsp whole coriander seeds
- ½ tsp jeera
- 7 bydagi red chillies (or Kashmiri red chillies)
- 5-6 methi seeds
- ¼ tsp hing
- ¼ cup fresh grated coconut
- 8 curry leaves
- 1 small onion chopped

For the sambar gravy

- 1 cup arhar dal washed and soaked in water for half an hour
- 1 tsp oil
- ½ tsp haldi
- 100 gm pearl or sambar onions peeled
- 1 tomato chopped
- 1 small ball tamarind soaked in half cup water for half an hour
- ½ tsp salt
- 1 tsp jaggery
- ½ tsp mustard seeds
- 8 curry leaves
- 1 tbsp chopped coriander leaves

Method

1. Boil the dal in a pressure cooker with salt and haldi for 12 minutes after the whistle. Once cool, remove and mash the dal well.

2. In the meant time prepare the masala. Heat 1 tsp oil in a pan. Add jeera and dhania seeds and fry for 2 minutes on low flame. Remove in a bowl. Add the red chillies and methi seeds and fry for 1 minute. Remove in the above bowl. Add the onion and fry till it is translucent. Remove in the bowl.
3. Add the curry leaves and grated coconut in the pan and fry for a minute. The coconut should not turn brown. Add the hing and put off the gas. Let it cool. Grind all the above roasted elements in a mixie with little water till you get a smooth paste.
4. Heat 1 tsp oil in a kadhai. Add the mustard seeds and fry till they splutter. Add the curry leaves.
5. Add the pearl onions and fry for 2 minutes on low flame. Add the tomatoes and fry for 1 minute.
6. Add the water from the soaked tamarind after squeezing the pulp. Cook for 1 minute.
7. Add 2 cups of water. Bring to a boil and add the ground sambar masala. Boil for 5 minutes on a medium flame. Add the boiled and mashed arhar dal, jaggery and continue simmering on low flame for 5-7 minutes.
8. Check for consistency, seasoning and salt.
9. Remove in a serving bowl and garnish with coriander leaves. Serve hot with rice, idli, dosa.

Tips:

1. Other vegetables that can be added to sambar include bhindi, pumpkin, brinjal, drumsticks and radish.
2. If you want to use store bought masala, I prefer MTR Sambar powder. I still use it sometimes, especially when I'm in a hurry

Mor Kuzhambu

My mother's recipe whenever excess curd was available at home -Mor Kuzhambu. It is like a South Indian kadhi.

Ingredients

- 1 tsp Arhar dal
- ½ tsp rice
- ½ tsp jeera
- 1 tsp whole dhania seeds
- ½ cup grated coconut
- 2 green chillies
- 100 gm white pumpkin cut into bite sized pieces
- 1 cup curd
- ½ tsp haldi
- ½ tsp salt or to taste
- 1 tsp oil
- ¼ tsp mustard seeds
- Hing – a pinch
- 8 curry leaves

Method

1. Soak arhar dal, jeera, whole dhania and raw rice in half a cup water. Keep for 30 minutes.
2. Drain the water and grind with the grated coconut, green chillies with a little water till you get a smooth paste.
3. Meanwhile boil the white pumpkin in water till done (approx. 10 minutes). Drain.
4. Whisk 1 cup curd with haldi till smooth. Add 1 cup water and salt. Whisk again.
5. Add boiled pumpkin, coconut spice paste to the curd. Place on medium flame on the gas, bring to boil. Reduce the flame to the minimum and simmer for 4 minutes.
6. Temper with 1 tsp oil, mustard seeds, hing and curry leaves.
7. Add the temper to the boiled mor kuzhambu.
8. Serve with steamed rice.

Kabuli Chana

My friend Mrs Lakshmi Ramakrishnan gave me this recipe. Simple and easy - no fuss recipe.

Ingredients

- 1 cup Kabuli chana
- ¼ tsp cooking soda
- 2 tea bags (for the dark brown colour)
- 3 dry amla (optional)
- 1 bayleaf (tejpatta)
- 2-3 cloves
- 1 stick cinnamon (2 cm long)
- 3 green cardamoms
- 1 tsp ghee
- ½ tsp salt or to taste
- 1 big onion
- 2 big tomatoes
- 4 garlic cloves
- 3 tsp oil
- 1 tsp jeera
- 2 tsp dhania powder
- 1 tsp jeera powder
- ½ tsp garam masala
- ½ tsp red chilli powder
- 2 tsp amchur
- ½ tsp pepper powder
- 1 tsp chaat masala
- 2 tsp chana masala – store bought
- ½ tsp kala namak

Method

1. Soak the Kabuli chana with soda overnight. Drain. Add fresh water to one inch above the chanas.
2. Boil the chana in an open cooker till the white froth appears on top.
3. Remove the froth. Add more water and pressure cook along with tejpatta, cloves, cinnamon, little salt, tea bags, cardamom and ghee. Close the lid of the cooker.

4. Boil it for 25 minutes after the whistle. Let it cool before opening the lid.
5. Grind the onion, tomatoes and garlic coarsely.
6. Heat oil. Add jeera and fry for one minute.
7. Add above ground onion-tomato-garlic paste and sauté till oil leaves pan.
8. Add garam masala, jeera powder, dhania powder, pepper powder, red chilli powder, amchur, chaat masala and chana masala. Sauté for 2 to 3 minutes.
9. Add the boiled chana after removing the tejpatta, tea bags, and whole spices.
10. Add kala namak. Mix well. Boil for five minutes on a medium flame. Check the seasonings and salt.
11. Mash a few chanas for a thick gravy. Serve with onion rings and ginger juliennes soaked in lime juice.

Tips

1. Tie the whole spices like clove, elaichi, cinnamon in a potli and boil. Remove and then proceed.

Sinful Punjabi Chole

My friend Dr. Kavita Sahai's mother-in-law Mrs. Rajendra Sahai used to make these chole, which we call sinful Punjabi chole at our house. It reminds my Delhi Walla husband of the chole he used to have at the street stalls of Delhi. It is a no onion, no garlic dish, full of the goodness of ghee and spices. Thank you Aunty and rest in peace.

Ingredients

- 2 cups Kabuli chana
- ¼ tsp cooking soda
- 2 tea bags (for the dark brown colour)
- 3 dry amla (optional)
- 5 cloves
- 1 stick cinnamon (2 cm long)
- 3-4 green cardamoms
- 3-4 black cardamoms
- 1 tsp jeera
- 2 tbsp whole dhania seeds
- ¼ tsp hing
- 5-6 red chillies
- 1 tsp whole peppercorns
- 1/8 tsp nutmeg powder
- 2 flowers javitri
- ½ tsp mustard seeds
- ½ tsp kalonji
- 3-4 methi seeds
- 1 tej patta
- Salt to taste
- Pinch of sugar
- 2-3 tsp amchur powder
- 4 tbsp ghee
- 2 green chillies slit
- 1 inch ginger julienned

Method

1. Soak the Kabuli chana with soda overnight. Drain. Add fresh water to one inch above the chanas.
2. Boil the chana in an open cooker till the white froth appears on top. Remove the froth.
3. Add more water and pressure cook along with little salt, tea bags and amla. Close the lid of the cooker. Boil it for 20-25 minutes after the whistle. Let it cool before opening the lid.
4. Drain the chanas and keep the chanas aside and the chana liquid separate. Cool. The liquid will thicken.
5. Heat a pan. Dry roast each of the above spices individually on low heat except kalonji and hing. This takes time. Give at least 2 minutes per spice. Then grind the roasted spices along with kalonji and hing. Sieve the roasted ground spices.
6. Put the chanas in a kadhai. Add julienned ginger and sliced green chilli on top.
7. Heat ghee in a small kadhai. Heat till it is smoking. Put off gas.
8. Add 1 tbsp hot ghee, 1 tbsp masala mix, 1 tbsp chana fluid on the chanas. Add amchur, salt and sugar. Mix well.
9. Keep repeating the ghee, masala mix and chana fluid till all the ghee finishes.
10. Mix in between. Then heat the kadhai with chanas. You may add chana water for more gravy or have it almost dry. Cook for 15 minutes on low flame.
11. The chanas will turn a deep brown. Check for seasonings.

Tips:

1. The ingredients have to be roasted on low flame, slowly and individually. I usually make it a day prior or while the chana is cooking. This takes time but is the heart of this chole.
2. The above spice mix would be adequate for 2 cups kabuli channa. This would serve 6-8 persons.

Dalma

My younger daughter Shivani was handed down this Oriya dal recipe by her mother-in-law Bandana Sahu. It is a healthy sumptuous dal with assorted vegetables.

Ingredients

- 1 tbsp raw papaya peeled and diced
- 1 tbsp white pumpkin peeled and diced
- 1 tbsp ridge gourd peeled and diced
- 1 tbsp potato peeled and diced
- 1 cup arhar dal soaked for half an hour
- Salt to taste
- ½ tsp haldi

For the masala

- 2 tsp jeera
- 2 red chillies
- 1 tej patta
- 4-5 peppercorns
- 1 tsp ghee

Method

1. Steam the diced vegetables for 5-6 minutes. You could use whatever vegetable is available.
2. Dry roast the ingredients under masala. Remove the tej patta and grind the rest.
3. Boil the arhar dal with salt and haldi in a pressure cooker for 12 minutes after the whistle. The dal should be well cooked.
4. Remove the dal in a pan. Add the vegetables and roasted and ground spices and tej patta. Simmer for 3-4 minutes.
5. Check seasoning.
6. Add 1 tsp of ghee on top and serve hot.

Rice

- Types of Rice and its cooking methods
  - Flavored Rice
  - Curd Rice
  - Jeera Rice
  - Ven Pongal
  - Sweet Pongal
- Vegetable Biryani -1
- Vegetable Biryani -2
  - Bisibele Bhath

Types of Rice its cooking methods

Types of rice I use:

- Basmati rice – for pulaos, Biryani, jeera rice
- Sona Masuri rice – for south Indian flavored rice like coconut rice, puliyogara, bisibele bhath, curd rice, pongals, chitranna
- Gobindbhog rice – exclusively for kheer
- Dosa rice – for dosa batter
- Parboiled rice – for dosa batter

General preparations:

- Wash the rice 4 to 5 times in water till the water appears clean.
- Drain and keep aside, covered, for half an hour.
- I have found that if the rice is kept soaked in water, sometimes it turns mushy or overcooked when boiled. Whereas, if it is drained and kept, it cooks just right.
- The amount of water needed for cooking rice would vary between the types of rice. In general, for Sona Masuri, use double the volume of water. For biryanis, I use 1 ½ the amount of water.
- Cooking times would also vary depending upon how you want the rice to be done. The following times are what I am comfortable with.

Cooking methods:
Pressure cooker:

- Add the rice in a pressure cooker compatible dish or directly in the cooker.
- Add double the amount of water.
- Bring to steam or whistle on a high flame.
- Reduce the flame and cook on a low flame for 3 -4 minutes.
- This method is useful for rice in daily meals or curd rice.

Open pan (1):

- Bring water to boil in an open pan. Add almost 5 to 6 times water as compared to the rice.
- Once it is completely boiling, then bring the flame to medium, and add the rice. Stir well. And cook uncovered for 8 to 10 minutes or until almost done.

- Drain the water and spread the rice on a plate till the grains are separate. Cool and use in the preparation.
- This method is useful for pulaos, biryani, and flavoured rice.

Open pan (2):

- Bring water to boil in an open pan. Add 1 ½ times water as compared to the rice. (e.g. for 1 cup rice, add 1 ½ cups of water)
- Reduce the flame to low medium.
- Cover and cook till the water has evaporated and the rice grains stand up in the pan. This would take 5 to 6 minutes. The rice grains should be almost done (80%) and separate.
- Cool and use for pulaos, biryani and flavored rice.

Flavoured Rice

On Makar Sankaranti, I usually make an array of flavored rice. And once a week, when my children were at school, their snack box contained one or the other type of flavored rice.

Chitranna (Lemon rice)
Ingredients

- 2 cups cooked rice or leftover rice (Sona Masuri)
- Salt to taste
- 2 tsp oil
- ½ tsp mustard seeds
- ½ tsp haldi
- 10 curry leaves
- 1 tsp urad dal
- 1 tsp channa dal
- 2 tbsp peanuts
- 1 green chilli chopped
- 2 tbsp coriander leaves chopped
- Juice of 2 lemons

Method

1. The rice should be just cooked (not mushy) and the grains should be separate. Bring the cooked rice to room temperature.
2. Heat the oil. Fry the peanuts till done. Remove the peanuts and keep aside.
3. In the same oil, temper with mustard seeds and fry till they crackle.
4. Add the dals and fry till they turn light brown.
5. Add the chilli, curry leaves and haldi and cook for half a minute.
6. Add 2 tsp of water and fry till the water has dried. This makes the dals a little soft.
7. Remove from flame.
8. Add the cooked rice, lemon juice, salt and mix thoroughly.
9. Serve, garnished with coriander leaves and fried peanuts.

• • •

Raw Mango rice

The ingredients are the same as chitranna rice except for:

1. Substitute the lemon juice with 3 tbsp of grated raw mango.
2. Fry the grated mango after addition of haldi as in the previous recipe.
3. The rest of the procedure remains the same.

• • •

Coconut Rice

The ingredients are the same as chitranna rice except for:

1. Substitute the lemon juice with 3-4 tbsp of freshly grated coconut, and add 2 red chillies instead of green chilli. Omit haldi.
2. The rest of the procedure remains the same.
3. Add the coconut to the rice after the tempering step and mix well.

• • •

Puliyogarai rice (tamarind rice)
Ingredients

- 2 cups cooked rice or left over rice (Sona Masuri)
- Salt to taste
- 2 tsp oil
- ½ tsp mustard seeds
- 10 curry leaves
- 1 tsp urad dal
- 1 tsp channa dal
- 2 tbsp peanuts
- 2-3 tbsp of MTR Puliogare powder mix

Method

1. The rice should be just cooked and the grains should be separate. Bring the cooked rice to room temperature.
2. Heat the oil. Fry the peanuts till done. Drain the peanuts and keep aside.
3. In the same oil, temper with mustard seeds and fry till they crackle.
4. Add the dals and fry till they turn light brown.
5. Add the curry leaves and cook for half a minute.
6. Add 2 tsp of water and fry till the water has dried. This makes the dals a little soft.
7. Add the Puliogare powder and fry for one minute.
8. Remove from flame.
9. Add the cooked rice, fried peanuts and salt and mix thoroughly.
10. Serve at room temperature.

Curd Rice

A refreshing light summer lunch.

Ingredients

- 2 cups cooked Sona Masuri rice or Ponni rice
- 1 ½ cups curd
- Salt to taste
- 2 inch piece of carrot grated
- 2 tbsp chopped coriander
- 1 green chilli chopped
- ½ inch ginger grated
- 6-7 curry leaves
- 2 tsp oil for tempering
- ½ tsp mustard seeds
- ½ tsp urad dal
- ½ tsp channa dal

Method

1. Mix the cooked rice with curd, carrot, chilli, ginger, coriander leaves and salt. It is ideal to mix it well using hands to achieve a uniform consistency. You may adjust the curd if the mixture appears too dry.
2. Heat oil in a small tempering pan. Once it is hot, add the mustard seeds and fry till they crackle. Add the urad and channa dal and fry till light brown. Add the curry leaves.
3. Pour this tempering over the prepared curd rice.
4. Serve chilled.

I like to have this rice with fried curd chillies (also called Mor milagai and available at all South Indian stores).

Jeera Rice

A simple flavourful rice. I had it at a Pune restaurant many moons back and make it when I want to jazz up plain leftover rice.

Ingredients:

- ½ cup Basmati rice
- 2 tsp cumin seeds
- 1 tbsp ghee
- 2 tbsp chopped coriander leaves
- Salt to taste

Method

1. Wash the rice thoroughly. Soak for 30 minutes and drain.
2. Boil 5 cups of water in a pan with ½ tsp salt.
3. Once it is a rolling boil, reduce the gas flame to medium and add the rice.
4. Stir well cook till almost done.
5. Drain the excess water and spread the rice on a plate.
6. Heat a frying pan.
7. Add ghee. When hot, reduce the flame to medium and add the cumin seeds.
8. Fry for a minute till they crackle.
9. Add the chopped coriander leaves and fry for one minute.
10. Add the rice. Adjust the salt. And fry for one minute. Serve hot.

Ven Pongal

This is a favorite South Indian breakfast dish. I make it during Makar Sankranti along with sweet pongal and flavoured rice.

Ingredients

- 1 cup Sona Masuri rice
- ¾ cup yellow Moong dal
- Salt to taste
- 3 tbsp ghee
- 1 tsp cumin seeds
- 1 inch ginger grated
- 1 tsp peppercorns
- 10 to 12 cashews, halved

Method

1. Wash the dal and rice and soak separately in water for 30 minutes.
2. Boil the dal and rice in the cooker in separate pans for 10-12 minutes.
3. Heat the ghee in a pan and keep on medium heat.
4. Fry the cashews till light brown. Remove from the pan and keep aside.
5. Add the cumin seeds and fry till they crackle. Then add the peppercorns.
6. Fry for a minute.
7. Add the ginger and stir for one minute.
8. Add the rice, dal and salt. Mix well and keep stirring on low flame.
9. Add water if necessary to reach a consistency of a thick gruel or khichdi.
10. Serve hot garnished with the fried cashews. You may optionally add 1 tsp of ghee to enhance the taste.

Sweet Pongal

Ingredients

- ¾ cup Sona Masuri rice
- ½ cup moong dal
- 1 cup grated jaggery
- 2 tbsp ghee
- 10-12 cashews, halved
- ½ tsp green cardamom powder

Method

1. Wash the dal and rice and soak separately in water for 30 minutes.
2. Boil the dal and rice in the cooker in separate pans for 10-12 minutes.
3. Heat the ghee in a pan and keep on medium heat.
4. Fry the cashews till light brown. Remove from the pan and keep aside along with the ghee.
5. Boil half a cup of water in a pan. Add the jaggery and cook on low flame till all the jaggery melts.
6. Cook for 5 minutes stirring in between.
7. Add the rice and dal. Mix well and keep stirring on low flame.
8. Add water if necessary to reach a consistency of a thick gruel or khichdi.
9. Add the cardamom powder and mix well.
10. Serve hot garnished with the fried cashews and ghee.

Vegetable Biryani

My friend Deepa Rajagopal is a very good cook. All her dishes are delectable. She introduced me to this veg biryani which is simple yet flavorful. A perfect Sunday lunch with raita and papad.

Vegetable Biryani-1:

Ingredients

- 1 cup Basmati rice
- 1 medium carrot chopped into half inch pieces
- 12-15 French beans chopped into half inch pieces
- 1 medium potato chopped into half inch pieces
- Half cup green peas
- 1 onion sliced
- 1 tomato chopped
- 1 inch ginger
- 6-8 cloves garlic
- 2 green chillies
- 3 tbsp mint leaves chopped
- 3 tbsp coriander leaves chopped
- ½ cup coconut milk
- Salt to taste
- ½ tsp haldi
- 2 tbsp oil
- 2 tbsp ghee
- Whole spices- 1 bay leaf, 5 cloves, 2 inch cinnamon, 4 green cardamoms, 2 black cardamoms, 1 star anise

Method

1. Wash the rice well. Drain and keep aside for half an hour.
2. Make a paste of the ginger, garlic and green chilli.
3. Heat the oil and ghee in a pan. Once hot, keeping it on medium flame, add the whole spices and fry for a minute or two.
4. Add the ginger-garlic-chilli paste and sauté for 3 minutes till the raw smell goes off.

5. Add the mint leaves. Fry for a minute.
6. Then add haldi and onion. Fry for 2 minutes.
7. Add the rest of the vegetables and tomatoes and fry for 2-3 minutes.
8. Add rice and salt and fry on a low flame for 2 minutes. Add the coriander leaves. Mix well.
9. Add 1 ½ cups of water and ½ cup coconut milk. Cover and cook for 8 -10 minutes or until done.

Tips

1. I usually make this in the rice cooker. After frying the rice in the pan, I transfer the mixture to a rice cooker, add the water and coconut milk and let it cook. This takes around 20 minutes.
2. If using a cooker, just 2 minutes after full steam is enough to cook it.

Vegetable Biryani-2:

This is a more elaborate biryani recipe but the results are delightful. I use store bought biryani masala powder and combine it with whole spices to give a better effect.

Ingredients
For rice

- 1 cup basmati rice
- Salt to taste
- 2 bay leaves
- 3 cloves
- 1 inch cinnamon
- 4-5 green cardamom
- 2 black cardamom

For Vegetable marination

- 1 carrot cut into 1 inch batons
- 10-12 French beans cut into 1 inch pieces
- 1 medium potato cut into 1 inch batons
- ½ cup green peas
- 2 large onions sliced
- 1 cup thick curd
- 3 tbsp chopped mint
- 3 tbsp chopped coriander leaves
- 1 inch ginger

- 6-8 cloves garlic
- 2 tsp Kashmiri red chilli powder
- ½ tsp haldi
- 2 tsp coriander powder
- 3 tbsp store bought Biryani masala powder
- 2 tbsp oil
- 2 tbsp ghee
- 10-12 strands saffron soaked in ¼ cup warm milk
- Few drops of Kewra water

Method
Rice:

1. Wash the rice well. Drain and keep aside for 30 minutes.
2. Boil 5 cups water in a pan. Add the rice along with the whole spices and salt.
3. Cook the rice till it is 80% done.
4. Drain and spread the rice on a plate to cool. The rice grains should be separate.

Vegetable marination:

1. Grind the ginger and garlic along with curd and biryani masala powder (store bought).
2. Add the vegetables to the above marinade along with 1 tbsp mint leaves. Keep aside for 15 minutes.
3. Heat oil in a pan. Fry the onion slices till brown. Drain and keep aside.
4. In the same oil, add the vegetables along with the marinade and cook covered till the vegetables are almost done. There should be gravy left. If it appears too dry add half a cup of water.
5. Add haldi, Kashmiri red chilli powder, coriander powder and fry for 2 minutes.

To assemble:

1. First place a layer of the cooked rice at the bottom of the pan or handi.
2. Add half the vegetables with gravy on top.
3. Add half of fried onions, 1 tbsp coriander and mint leaves on top.
4. Dot with a few drops of saffron milk and drizzle one tbsp ghee on it.
5. Repeat the rice, vegetable layers and remaining mint and coriander leaves. Pour the remaining saffron milk and spread the remaining fried onions on top. Put a few drops of kewra water and drizzle 1 tbsp of ghee over the assembled rice.
6. Cover with a tight fitting lid. Preferably, place the pan on an iron tawa on low heat and cook for 10-15 minutes. Remove from the gas. And keep aside for 8-10 minutes.
7. Serve hot with a raita of your choice.

Bisibele Bhath

A favorite meal at our house. My go-to dish when I feel lazy, resorting to this one meal lunch or dinner. I usually serve it with papad or khara boondi and a bowl of curd. The secret to a lip-smacking bisibele bhath is ghee. Use it generously.

Ingredients

- ½ cup Sona Masuri rice
- ½ cup arhar dal
- Half carrot, diced
- 10 avarekkai or broad beans, cut into half inch pieces (not always available, so I use French beans instead)
- 10 French beans, cut into half inch pieces
- 1 small potato diced
- 1 onion chopped
- 1 tomato chopped
- 10 curry leaves
- 2 tbsp cashews halved
- ½ tsp mustard seeds
- ½ tsp haldi
- 2 tbsp MTR Bisibele Bhath masala powder (I use only this brand)
- 1 small ball of tamarind soaked in water
- 1 tsp oil
- 3 tbsp ghee
- Salt to taste

Method

1. Wash and soak the rice and dals separately for an hour.
2. I use a pressure cooker with separator pans in which I add the dal and rice separately.
3. Boil the rice with 1 cup water till well done.
4. Boil the dal with 1 ½ cups water with salt and haldi for at least 12 minutes.
5. Steam the vegetables – carrot, beans and potato for 5 minutes.
6. In a pan, heat the oil. Fry the cashews till light brown. Drain and keep aside.
7. Add mustard seeds to the same oil and fry till they crackle. Add the curry leaves.
8. After a minute, add the onion and sauté till transparent. Add the tomato and fry for 3 minutes.

9. Squeeze the water from the tamarind and add the juice. Fry for 2 minutes until the raw smell disappears. Add the MTR Bisibele bhath powder and fry for 2 minutes.
10. Add the steamed vegetables, dal and rice. Mix well. Add salt to taste and 2 tbsp of ghee.
11. The consistency of this dish is like khichdi, slightly mushy. So add water to bring to the right consistency.
12. Cook on low flame for 5 minutes stirring occasionally.
13. Take the rice out in a serving dish, garnish with the fried cashews. Add the remaining tbsp of ghee on top.
14. Serve immediately with papad and curd.

Breads

- Puri and Luchi
- Stuffed Paratha
- Jowar Thalipeeth
- Pangi
- Thepla
- Matar Kachori with Aloo Rassa
- Aloo Kachori

Puri and Luchi

My puris never turned out ideal; they were either too crisp or too soft. Somewhere in 1999, I attended a talk by Master Chef Sanjeev Kapoor along with my husband. During the audience interaction, I asked him the best way to make puris. To which, he asked "Is that your husband sitting next to you?" I said yes and then he said "The next time you make puris, ask your husband to knead the dough!" And believe me, the puris did turn out great using this magical technique.

Puri
Ingredients

- 1 cup atta
- 3 tsp warm oil
- Salt to taste
- Water to knead
- Oil for frying

Method

1. Mix the salt and oil in the atta. Add water and make a stiff dough. Knead well – this is the trick to making good puris.
2. Let the dough rest for half an hour.
3. Heat oil in a kadai. Test with a small ball of dough-it should rise immediately. Turn the flame to medium.
4. Divide the dough into lemon sized balls. Roll each into a 4 inch diameter circle (do not use flour for rolling, use oil).
5. Fry the puris on medium heat. Gently press the puri after putting it in oil. This helps the puri to puff up uniformly.
6. Once puffed up, then invert and cook the other side till it is pale brown in color. Drain and serve hot.

Luchi

My earliest memory of having these feathery light luchis was at my school friend Smeeta's house. Her mother Mrs. Shanta would lovingly give us two luchis and cham-cham in the evenings.

Ingredients

- Maida 1 cup or you could use a mixture of atta and maida
- Oil 3 tsp
- Salt to taste
- Oil for frying

Method

1. Mix the maida, salt and oil and rub with finger tips. Add water slowly to make a dough which is not too stiff. Let it rest for half an hour.
2. Roll out discs around 4 inch diameter but thinner than puris. Fry in moderately hot oil as you would for puris.

Stuffed Paratha

Ingredients
For the dough

- 1 ½ cup atta
- Pinch of salt
- 1 tsp ghee or oil
- Water to knead
- Oil for the tawa frying

Method

- Make a soft dough combining the above ingredients.
- Rest the dough for 15 minutes and then use. Make 4 balls.
- Roll one ball into a small circle 5" diameter. Put the stuffings as desired in the centre. Close the edges. Roll again till you get an 8 or 9 inch paratha, dust with flour in between the rollings.
- Cook on a medium hot tawa for 2 minutes. Turn over. Spread 1 tsp oil on the top. After one minute, turn over. Spread oil. Cook till light brown specs appear.
- Serve hot with butter, mint chutney, pickle and curd.

Stuffings:
Paneer
Ingredients

- 100 gm paneer grated
- 1 finely chopped onion
- 1 finely chopped green chilli
- 1 tbsp chopped coriander leaves
- Salt to taste

Combine the above ingredients. Divide into 4 portions and use for stuffing.

• • •

Aloo
Ingredients

- 2 medium sized potatoes boiled, peeled and mashed

- 1 finely chopped onion
- 1 finely chopped green chilli
- ½ tsp ajwain
- 1 tbsp chopped coriander leaves
- Salt to taste
- ½ tsp amchur powder

Combine the above ingredients. Divide into 4 portions and use for stuffing.

• • •

Cauliflower
Ingredients

- 1 small cauliflower grated
- 1 finely chopped onion
- 1 finely chopped green chilli
- 1 tbsp chopped coriander leaves
- Salt to taste

Combine the above ingredients. Divide into 4 portions and use for stuffing.

• • •

Cabbage / Radish
Ingredients

- 1 small cabbage or 1 medium radish grated
- 1 finely chopped green chilli
- Half tsp ajwain
- 1 tbsp chopped coriander leaves
- Salt to taste

Method

1. Sprinkle salt on the grated cabbage or radish. Keep aside for 20 minutes.
2. Then squeeze out all the water. Add rest of the ingredients as above and mix well.
3. Divide into 4 parts and proceed as above. Remember that cabbage and radish retain water, so the rolling must be done fast or else it will stick to the dough.

• • •

Spring onion and cheese
Ingredients

- 100 gm spring onions

- 50 to 70 gm cheese grated
- Salt to taste
- ½ tsp freshly ground pepper
- Chop the greens and bulb of the spring onions finely.

Mix the above and use for stuffing

Palak Paneer
Ingredients

- 250 gm palak – use only leaves
- Atta as required
- Salt to taste

Method

1. Clean the palak leaves.
2. Blanch in boiling water for 3 minutes.
3. Drain well, dry with kitchen towels. Cool and puree.
4. Add atta, salt and make a dough. Add atta little by little into the puree till you get a firm dough.
5. Stuff it with paneer filling as mentioned above.

• • •

Methi
Ingredients

- Methi leaves I cup
- Atta 1 cup
- Salt to taste
- 1 tsp oil
- Water to knead

Method

1. Chop the methi leaves. Sprinkle salt and leave for half an hour. Squeeze out the water. Add atta, oil and make a dough with water. Roll into a chapati and cook on a tawa with oil.

• • •

Pudina
Ingredients

- Pudina leaves 1 cup chopped
- Atta 1 cup
- Salt to taste
- Oil 1 tsp

Method

1. To the chopped pudina leaves, add atta, salt, oil and make a dough with water.
2. Roll into a roti and cook on a tawa with oil on both sides.

Jowar Thalipeeth

I was introduced to Thalipeeth after marriage. And I used to make it with store bought Thalipeeth Bhajani powder. However, during a recent visit to my cousin Rajeev's house, we had delicious Jowar Thalipeeth for breakfast. I got a basic recipe from his cook and have tried many proportions of the flours and finally settled on the following recipe.

Ingredients (for 5-6 thalipeeths)

- 1 cup jowar atta
- ½ cup besan
- ½ cup whole wheat flour (atta)
- 1 medium onion, finely chopped
- 1 green chilli chopped
- Half a small cucumber, grated and squeezed
- 2 tbsp chopped coriander leaves
- ½ tsp haldi
- Salt to taste
- ½ tsp dhania powder
- ½ tsp jeera powder
- 2 tsp oil (plus more oil for the tawa)
- 1/3 cup thick curd

Method

1. Mix all the above ingredients to make a medium stiff dough with water. Let it rest for 15 minutes.
2. Heat a tawa.
3. Make 6 balls from the dough. Roll out each ball into a 6 to 8 inch circle, 2 mm thick.
4. If it is difficult to roll, then place the dough ball on a plastic sheet or aluminium foil and press gently into a circle.
5. Place the thalipeeth on the tawa and cook on low to medium flame. After brown specks appear on one side, turn over. Spread oil on the cooked sides.
6. Repeat until the thalipeeth is fully cooked. This would take 4-5 minutes.
7. Serve hot with white butter, chutney or pickle and curd.

Pangi

This was taught by my mother-in-law and happens to be my husband's favorite. Invariably, when I used to make white butter from malai at home, Pangi was on the dinner table menu.

Ingredients

- 1 cup rice flour
- 2 to 2 ½ tbsp powdered sugar
- ¼ tsp salt
- Pinch of cooking soda
- 1 cup full cream milk (room temperature)
- Banana leaves. Cut from the central vein into 10 inch pieces. Two such pieces are required for one Pangi

Method

1. Mix the rice flour with sugar, salt and cooking soda.
2. Gradually add the milk, mixing well till you get a thick batter (Adjust the milk quantity for a thick batter).
3. Let it rest for half an hour. Heat a tawa.
4. Take one banana leaf, shiny side facing up. Pour one ladle of the Pangi batter on the center of the leaf.
5. Spread till you get a circle around 3 mm thick.
6. Cover with the second banana leaf, shiny side facing down.
7. Place this on the heated tawa. Cook on a medium flame.
8. After 2 minutes, the bottom leaf would have shrunk and have brown specks.
9. Flip it over and cook for another two minutes.
10. The end point is that the tops of the Pangi should be lightly roasted and brown.
11. Serve hot with a dollop of white butter and green chilli pickle.

Tips

1. Fresh unboiled pasteurized milk is preferred for the best results.
2. Also, the fresher the rice powder, the better the pangi's turn out.

Thepla

I find theplas a filling breakfast dish, especially in winters, when fresh methi is available. I usually serve it with Chunda (a sweet tangy grated mango pickle).

Ingredients

- 1 cup atta
- 1/3 cup besan
- Salt to taste
- ½ tsp haldi
- 1 cup methi leaves
- ½ tsp red chilli powder
- ½ cup curd
- 2 tbsp oil (plus oil for tawa frying)

Method

1. Chop the methi leaves. Sprinkle some salt and keep it aside for 10 minutes. Wash the excess salt and squeeze the leaves till all the water is removed.
2. Mix all the above ingredients into a medium to soft dough using water.
3. Let it rest for 15 minutes.
4. Divide the dough into 6 balls.
5. Roll each ball into a circle 6-8 inches in diameter, 2 mm thick, using flour for dusting.
6. Heat a tawa.
7. Place a thepla on the tawa and cook one side for 1 minute on medium flame.
8. Turn the thepla over and cook the other side.
9. Spread oil on the first cooked side and flip it on the tawa to cook further.
10. Repeat for the second side. The thepla should have brown specks on it.
11. Serve hot or cold with chunda.

Matar Kachori with Aloo Rassa

Mrs. Shyamali Chatterjee (my friend Dr. Chandreyee's mother) produced these delicious Matar Kachoris with a simple potato gravy for tea while I was visiting her in Bangalore. This became one of the Sunday breakfast treats at our house.

Ingredients
For the dough

- 1 cup atta
- 2 tsp oil
- Salt to taste

For the filling

- 1 cup green peas-boiled
- ½ tsp jeera powder
- ½ tsp garam masala
- Salt to taste
- 2 tsp oil
- 1 green chilli chopped.
- Oil for deep frying

Method

1. Combine all the items under dough. Knead into a stiff dough with water. Let it rest for 15 minutes.
2. Meanwhile, puree the boiled peas and green chilli.
3. Heat 2 tsp oil in a pan. Add the pureed peas, jeera powder, salt and garam masala.
4. Fry for 3 to 4 minutes till the mixture turns almost dry.
5. Cool the mixture and make small lemon sized balls.
6. Divide the dough into 8-10 balls.
7. Roll into a 3 cm diameter circle. Place the cooked pea's ball in the center. Bring the edges together.
8. Roll again into a 4 inch circle.
9. Fry in medium hot oil on both sides, till brown specks appear.
10. Serve hot with a simple potato gravy (aloo rassa)

• • •

Aloo Rassa

Ingredients

- 2 medium potatoes boiled, crumbled coarsely
- Salt to taste
- 1 tsp oil
- 1 onion chopped
- 2 tomatoes chopped
- ½ tsp chopped ginger
- ½ tsp cumin seeds
- ½ tsp garam masala
- ½ tsp haldi
- 1 tbsp coriander leaves chopped

Method

1. Heat the oil. Add the cumin seeds and fry for a minute. Add haldi.
2. Add the onions and ginger and fry on medium flame till the onion turns translucent.
3. Add the chopped tomatoes and cook till the tomatoes turn mushy.
4. Add the crumbled potatoes, garam masala, salt and 1 cup water.
5. Cook on low flame till you get a thick gravy.
6. Garnish with coriander leaves.
7. Serve hot with Matar Kachori.

Aloo Kachori

Another one of my Sunday breakfast specials. I serve this with Bengali tomato chutney.

Ingredients
For the dough

- 1 cup atta
- 2 tsp oil
- Salt to taste

For the filling

- 2 medium potatoes- boiled and mashed
- ½ tsp jeera powder
- ½ tsp garam masala
- ½ tsp red chilli powder
- Salt to taste
- Oil for deep frying

Method

1. Combine all the items under dough. Knead into a stiff dough with water. Let it rest for 15 minutes.
2. Combine all items under filling well. Make small lemon sized balls.
3. Divide the dough into 8 -10 balls.
4. Roll the ball into a 4 cm diameter circle. Place the stuffing ball in the center. Bring the edges together.
5. Roll again into a 4 inch circle.
6. Fry in medium hot oil on both sides, till brown specks appear.
7. Serve hot with Bengali tomato chutney.

Sweets and Desserts

- Besan Ladoo
- Chirote
- Gajar Halwa
- Shahi Tukda
- Sooji Halwa
- Shrikhand
- Rice Kheer
- Seviyan Kheer
- Phirni
- Modak
- Kulfi
- Mishti Doi
- Bhappa Doi
- Sandesh
- Fruit Yoghurt
- Vanilla Ice Cream
- Mango Mastani
- Chocolate Cake
- Custard-Chocolate Sauce-Biscuit Pudding
- Choco Lava cake
- Tiramisu
- Apple pie

Besan Ladoo

My older daughter Divya's all-time favorite and a Diwali staple in our house. My husband also has grown up on these ladoos and cannot resist eating them.

Ingredients

- 1 cup besan
- 1 cup powdered sugar
- 1/3 cup ghee
- 1 tsp elaichi powder
- ¼ tsp jaiphal powder
- ¼ cup milk
- ¼ cup raisins

Method

1. Place the ghee in a heavy bottomed pan and heat.
2. On a low flame, fry the besan in the ghee till it turns golden brown stirring very frequently. The mixture should look a pale brown and like a thick liquid. The raw smell of besan should disappear. This process will take 20-30 minutes and there are no shortcuts for this.
3. When done, sprinkle milk over the mixture gradually and mix it after each sprinkle.
4. Remove the besan on a plate and spread. While still warm, sprinkle the powdered sugar evenly all over the besan. Add the elaichi and jaiphal powder and raisins.
5. Using the tips of fingers, gradually mix in the sugar with the besan till it is uniform.
6. Take a small lime sized ball of the besan-sugar mix. Place it on the palm and rotate the palm in a circular motion till you get uniform balls.
7. Cool and store.

Chirote

I like making Chirote for Diwali. It is so light and airy and full of crunch.

Ingredients

- 1 cup maida
- Pinch of salt
- 2 tbsp ghee
- Oil for deep frying
- 3 tbsp powdered sugar

Method

1. Heat 1 tbsp ghee. Add it to maida. Add the salt. Make a stiff dough with water. Cover with a moist cloth and keep aside for half an hour.
2. Divide the dough into 6 small balls.
3. Roll out 3 balls into a flat roti. The roti's should be rolled as thin as possible.
4. Mix 1 tbsp ghee with a tsp of powdered sugar.
5. Spread ½ tsp of ghee-sugar mixture over one roti.
6. Place a roti on top of the above and repeat with the ghee-sugar mixture.
7. Place another roti on top and repeat.
8. Make a tight roll with the three stacked rotis. Cut into half cm slices.
9. Repeat with the other 3 balls of dough.
10. Flatten each slice lightly with a rolling pin to 2 inch discs.
11. Heat oil in a frying pan. On a medium heat deep fry the flattened slices.
12. The slices will separate and resemble flower petals.
13. Remove and drain on a kitchen towel.
14. Sprinkle powdered sugar on each Chirote while still warm.
15. Store in an airtight container.

Gajar Halwa

An eternal winter favorite. It tastes especially good with red carrots. This is usually made in a kadhai with periodic stirring. However, I make it in the rice cooker till almost done and use the kadhai only in the last 10 minutes.

Ingredients

- 1 kg red carrots
- 1 litre full cream milk
- 10 tbsp sugar
- 3 tbsp ghee plus 2 tsp ghee
- 5 elaichi powdered finely
- 15 kismis soaked
- 15 cashews halved
- 10 almonds, soaked and peeled and finely sliced

Method

1. Peel and grate the carrots in the wide side of the grater.
2. Put it in the rice cooker.
3. Add 1 litre milk to the rice cooker and switch on.
4. (The above two steps can be done in a heavy bottomed kadhai but it has to be stirred periodically every 3 minutes or so).
5. Once the milk has reduced and is just coating the carrots, remove in a kadhai.
6. Add the sugar and cook till the mixture is almost dry.
7. Then add 3 tbsp ghee and stir and cook till the mixture is glossy and almost dry.
8. Heat 2 tsp ghee in a small pan. Fry the cashews till light brown. Remove. Fry the kismis for 30 seconds. Remove.
9. Add the kaju, kismis and almonds to the gajar halwa. Add the powdered elaichi. Mix well.
10. Serve hot.

Shahi Tukda

(makes 16 squares)

My take on the delightful Hyderabadi dish.

Ingredients

- 4 slices day old bread
- Sugar half cup
- 3 elaichi powdered
- Oil for frying

For Rabdi

- Milk – half litre full cream
- 5 tbsp sugar
- Kewra – 4 drops
- Saffron – a few strands

Method
Tukda

1. Cut bread into 4 pieces each with edges removed.
2. Deep fry in oil till brown.
3. Drain on a kitchen towel.
4. Meanwhile make the sugar syrup with half cup sugar and one and a half cups water. Boil for 3 minutes.
5. Soak the fried bread in the sugar syrup for 2 minutes. Remove and place on a serving plate

Rabri

1. Boil milk till it reduces to one third and becomes thick.
2. Add the sugar and mix well.
3. Add kewra.
4. Cool.
5. Put one tsp of Rabri on each tukda.
6. Top with 2 strands of saffron.
7. Chill and serve.

Sooji Halwa (Sheera)

After a hawan, my neighbour used to send the delicious prasad of halwa and kala channa. The best halwa I've ever tasted. One day I cornered the cook and got the recipe handed down by late Mrs. Airy.

Ingredients

- 1 cup sooji
- ½ cup ghee
- 1 cup sugar
- 3 cups water
- 1 tbsp kismis
- 1 tbsp cashew
- 3 elaichi powdered

Method:

1. Heat ghee. Fry sooji in it on low flame till ghee separates and the raw flavor disappears.
2. In the meantime, heat the water with sugar and kismis.
3. Add it to the sooji mixture. Stir continuously till thick and done.
4. Add the powdered elaichi.
5. Garnish with cashews fried in ghee.

Shrikhand

An eternal Maharashtrian favourite. I make it for Diwali, birthdays and for any celebration. Traditionally made with a Shrikhand machine, I use the hand mixer which gives as good results or even better.

Ingredients

- 2 litres full cream milk.
- 5 tbsp powdered sugar
- ¼ tsp salt
- ½ cup Milk (may require slightly more)
- 5 elaichi powdered
- Pinch of powdered nutmeg (jaiphal)
- 5 drops of yellow food colouring
- ¼ tsp saffron soaked in half cup of warm milk

Method

1. Boil milk and cool. Strain and set curd.
2. Hang curd in a cotton cloth for 3-4 hours if weather is not too hot. Or else 1-2 hrs in very hot summer days. This is called chakka.
3. In a bowl, beat the chakka with a hand mixer with an equal quantity of powdered sugar and ¼ tsp salt. The sugar is to be added gradually. Initially add less and adjust to taste – it should not be too sweet. If the chakka is too thick, beat with milk for desired consistency of thick custard.
4. Finely powder 5 elaichi, pinch of nutmeg and add to the above along with the yellow colour.
5. Soak saffron in warm milk for half hour and add to the above in end. This is the standard Shrikhand. Chill and serve.

Tips:

1. The Shrikhand thickens after refrigeration. So you may make it slightly more liquid initially.
2. For those picky eaters who do not like elaichi particles, here is my solution.
3. After crushing the elaichi and nutmeg, put it in half a cup of warm milk. Leave for half an hour. Strain and add to the beaten chakka.

Rice Kheer

After reaching Kolkata, I came to know that the locals use Gobindbhog rice for kheer. It is a short grained, aromatic rice grown in West Bengal. The kheer turns out creamy and delicious. It tastes better with palm jaggery which is available from Nov.

Ingredients:

- ½ cup or 5 tbsp Gobindbhog rice
- 1 lit full cream milk
- 12 tbsp sugar
- ¼ tsp cardamom powder
- 10 strands of saffron soaked in 1 tbsp of warm milk
- 10 kismis soaked in water

Method:

1. Wash the rice. Soak in water for half an hour.
2. Heat the milk till it starts boiling. Continue to simmer for 10 to 15 minutes.
3. Drain the water from the rice and add the rice to the simmering milk. Cook on low to medium flame for at least 20 minutes till the rice is cooked and the kheer looks thick.
4. Add the sugar and cook for another 5 minutes.
5. Drain the kismis and add to the kheer.
6. Put off the gas.
7. Add the cardamom powder and mix well.
8. Add the soaked saffron along with the milk.
9. Cool and serve.

Seviyan Kheer

A kheer which can be whipped up quickly. This can be made with thicker seviyan like Bambino or MTR also.

Ingredients

- 1 cup thin seviyan broken into 1 inch pieces
- 2 cups full cream milk
- 2 tsp ghee
- ½ cup sugar
- ½ tsp cardamom powder
- 10 raisins
- 10 cashews halved
- ½ tsp kewra essence

Method

1. Heat 1 tsp ghee in a pan. Roast the seviyan on a medium flame till light brown.
2. Add milk to the above and stir well till it thickens. Cook for 4-5 minutes on a low flame.
3. Add sugar and mix well. Adjust the consistency with more milk if required. Cook on a low flame for 2-3 minutes.
4. Let it cool.
5. Meanwhile heat the remaining 1 tsp ghee in a small pan. Fry the cashews. Remove when light brown. Then fry the raisins. Add to the kheer.
6. Add the cardamom powder and kewra. Mix well.
7. Serve cold or warm.

Phirni

This is a simple dish to make. Children especially love it.

Ingredients

- 5 tbsp rice soaked for half an hour. Drained and ground to a coarse paste.
- 1 litre milk preferably full cream milk
- ¾ cup sugar
- ½ tsp cardamom powder
- Few strands of saffron

Method 1:

1. Boil milk and keep it on simmer for 3-4 minutes.
2. Add ground rice paste little by little, stirring well to avoid lumps.
3. Stir on low flame until thick and the rice is cooked.
4. Add sugar and cook till the sugar dissolves.
5. Add cardamom powder. Mix well.
6. Garnish with saffron strands.
7. Serve chilled.

Method 2

1. After soaking the rice for half an hour, drain well on a kitchen towel. Keep aside for 20 minutes.
2. Grind without water till you get a coarse powder.
3. Follow the rest of steps as above.

Modak

Lord Ganesha's favourite food, made on every Ganesh Chaturthi at my house. My mother's recipe, which I have followed diligently for all these years. Although not really appreciated by my daughters, I have included this, in the hope that they follow this tradition.

Ingredients

- 1 cup rice powder
- 1 tsp ghee
- ¼ tsp salt
- 1 ½ cups water

Filling

- 1 cup grated coconut
- 1 cup jaggery
- ½ tsp elaichi powder
- 1 tsp ghee

Method
Filling

1. Heat 1 tsp ghee in a pan.
2. Add the coconut and jaggery and cook on a low flame for 8-10 minutes till the water evaporates and the mixture is a little dry. Add the elaichi powder and keep aside to cool.

For the covering:

1. Bring 1 ½ cups water to a boil. Add ghee and salt to it.
2. Keeping it on a low flame, add the rice powder gradually and mix well till a dough is formed.
3. Put off the gas. Keep covered for 5 minutes. While still warm, place the rice dough on a plate and knead well.
4. If the dough appears dry, you may add a little warm water and or ghee to make a smooth dough.
5. Divide the dough into lemon shaped balls.

6. Place one ball on a greased palm and with the other hand pat into a small circle. The circle should not be too thick or thin. Make pleats of the edges.
7. Place one teaspoon full of the filling in the centre. Gradually bring in the edges to form a dumpling.
8. I use a Modak mould to make modaks.
9. Place the modaks on a greased plate in a steamer and steam for 12-15 minutes.
10. Let it cool. Remove and cover with a moist cloth till serving time.

Tips

1. The fresher the rice powder, the better is the Modak covering.
2. With the above proportions of covering, I make around 15 modaks in my aluminium mould – 5 cm size.

Kulfi

My friend Arti Chaturvedi taught me this simple trick of adding bread to the kulfi mixture. This gives a nice creamy texture to the kulfi.

Ingredients:

- 1 litre full cream milk
- ¾ cup sugar
- 2 bread slices with edges removed and broken into pieces
- ½ tsp cardamom powder
- 15 strands saffron soaked in 2 tbsp of warm milk

Method:

1. Boil the milk till it is reduced to three-quarters.
2. Add the bread pieces and sugar.
3. Stir well for 5 minutes on a low flame.
4. Remove from the flame and let it cool.
5. Churn it in a wet grinder of the mixie till it is smooth.
6. Add the cardamom powder and saffron.
7. Pour into kulfi moulds or a covered glass container.
8. Freeze until firm.
9. Keep the container or mould out at room temperature for 2 minutes before serving the kulfi.

Mishti Doi

After our posting to Kolkata, we noticed that Mishti doi seemed to be available at every shop. I decided to try my hand at it. After many versions, hits and trials, I finally tweaked my recipe and found that this one gave consistent results.

Ingredients

- 1 lit full cream milk
- ¾ cup sugar (replace in winter with ¾ cup Nolen gur)
- Half cup thick curd (100 ml)

Method

1. First hang the curd in a muslin cloth for half an hour.
2. Boil the milk and continue boiling till it is half in volume.
3. When the milk is almost done, add half a cup of sugar and cook till sugar dissolves.
4. Heat a thick bottomed pan. Keep it on low flame. Add the remaining sugar (¼ cup) and stirring occasionally, caramelize the sugar till it is just brown. Put off the gas.
5. Add the thickened milk to the sugar. This is the tricky part. It will bubble furiously. Use a whisk and continue whisking the milk and caramel till it is mixed thoroughly.
6. Cool the milk mixture till it is warm to touch (a little more warm than what we would use for setting curd).
7. Take the hung curd. Add to the milk mixture. Mix thoroughly with a whisk.
8. Pour into the earthen pot through a sieve.
9. Cover and let it set for 6 to 8 hours in a warm place.
10. Enjoy the flavors of Bengal.

Tips:

1. The best results are with an earthen pot. Glazed ceramic or steel bowls do not give the same consistency.
2. The scary part is while adding the milk to the caramel and the mixture bubbles furiously. You could use mittens during this step to protect your hand.

3. The temperature has to be constantly maintained at around 40 °C. I do this by first warming my earthen pot in an oven around 60 °C for ten minutes. Remove the pot from the oven, pour in the dahi mixture. And then, I cover the pot with a thick cloth and keep it undisturbed for 6 to 8 hours (depending upon the weather).
4. I use only half the sugar for making the caramel. I found that this optimises the light beige colour and flavour.
5. In winters in Kolkata, the sugar is replaced by Nolen gur. The process of using caramel is avoided.

Bhappa Doi

My friend Mitali Nandi taught me this easy dessert. It is a no fail dessert and absolutely divine. Have it chilled on a warm summer evening

This is for a 8 inch diameter round dish

Ingredients

- 1 tin milkmaid (400 ml)
- 400 ml thick curd
- 400 ml milk
- Rose petals for decoration (optional)

Method:

1. Preheat the oven to 150 ℃.
2. Empty the milkmaid in a bowl.
3. Add the milk and curd to it.
4. Beat well with a hand mixer. Pour the mixture in an oven proof glass dish.
5. Reduce the oven temperature to 100 ℃.
6. Bake the above mixture at 100 ℃ for 1 to 1 ½ hours, uncovered.
7. Let it cool in the oven and then refrigerate.
8. Decorate with rose petals (optional).

Sandesh

My friend Dr. Manoshi taught me this recipe and Dr. Chandreyee gifted the wooden moulds to make it. Sandesh has always been a family favorite.

Ingredients

- 1 litre full cream milk
- Juice of 2 lemons
- 4 tbsp powdered sugar
- ¼ tsp powdered cardamom powder
- Oil to grease the moulds

Method

1. Bring the milk to boil. Reduce the gas and add the lemon juice and stir well. The milk should start curdling.
2. Take the milk off the gas and keep stirring for a minute till you see the whey separate.
3. Keep this covered for 2 minutes.
4. Drain the chenna through a thin cotton cloth and wash with water to remove the lemon flavor.
5. Squeeze out the remaining water. Keep the chenna with the cloth under a heavy weight object (like mortar or a filled tin) for half an hour.
6. Knead the chenna with the heel of the palm. This is a very crucial step. Knead for at least 5-7 minutes till the mixture is smooth and creamy.
7. Add the powdered sugar and powdered cardamom and continue kneading for another 5 minutes.
8. Heat a heavy bottomed pan. Add the kneaded chenna on low flame and keep stirring for 15 minutes.
9. Remove from the gas. Make small balls and shape it in the greased moulds.

Tips

1. Kneading the chenna is the most important step in preparation of Sandesh.
2. If you don't have the moulds, make small balls and flatten them.
3. Saffron soaked in milk can also be used to decorate the Sandesh balls.
4. The Sandesh is best eaten within a day or two.

Fruit Yoghurt

Many years back, while on a cruise on the river Rhine, we had a sumptuous lunch followed by this refreshing dessert. This is my version of the same.

Ingredients: (serves 4)

- 2 litres full cream milk set into curd Or alternatively, buy 2 litres thick curd
- 5 tbsp powdered sugar
- ½ tsp vanilla essence (Ossoro)
- A few drops of yellow food colouring to get a light yellow colour
- 2 apples peeled and diced
- 1 cup seedless grapes
- 2 medium mangoes peeled and diced
- 1 banana sliced
- 1 tin fruit cocktail drained
- I small tin canned pineapple (optional), drained and cut into half inch pieces
- 1 small tin cherries deseeded (optional), drained, deseeded

Method

1. Hang the curd in a cloth and let it drain for 2 to 3 hours. We don't want the hung curd to be dry. In summer, hang for less than 2 hours.
2. Take the hung curd in a bowl.
3. Add the powdered sugar, vanilla essence and beat till smooth and creamy. In case it looks too dry or thick, add some milk. Add a few drops of yellow food colour till it looks a pale yellow.
4. Add the drained fruit cocktail and other fruits. Mix well and chill.

Tips:

1. Do not add citrus fruits like orange, raw pineapple etc. The mixture turns bitter.

Vanilla Ice Cream

My husband's cousin Dr. Sandhya Khare and my friend Dr. Anagha Agrawal had treated me to this home-made ice-cream at almost the same time. It was so creamy and I could not believe that it was made at home. Both their recipes were identical. So after some procrastination, I bought an ice cream maker (Kitchenif) from Amazon. After that, there has been no looking back. There is always ice cream in the freezer on all summer days. The 2 powders used here are GMS and CMC. These are not harmful and are used as stabilisers and also used in commercial ice-creams. The alternative to these is egg, but I don't make ice creams with egg. These powders are available in department stores and also online.

Ingredients

- ½ lit full cream milk
- ¼ cup cold milk
- 1 cup (200 ml) sugar
- 1 ½ tbsp GMS
- ¼ tsp CMC
- 1 ½ tbsp cornflour
- 2 tbsp milk powder
- 1 tsp vanilla essence (I use Ossoro brand French vanilla for a mild flavour)
- 200 ml cream (1 tetrapak)

Method

1. Boil milk in a heavy bottomed pan. Add the sugar and boil till sugar dissolves.
2. Let it simmer for 5 minutes.
3. Mix the milk powder, cornflour, GMS and CMC in half a cup of cold milk. And add to above.
4. Stir continuously on a low flame till the mixture thickens and coats the back of the spoon.
5. Remove from fire and cool. Strain through a sieve.
6. Add 200 ml of cream and vanilla essence and whisk lightly. Refrigerate overnight.
7. In the meantime, take the inner container of the ice cream maker and chill in freezer at the minimum possible temp (around minus 20 to 23°C) for 24 hours.
8. Start the churner, pour the chilled ice cream mixture and put on the churner for 20 to 25 minutes.
9. You will be able to see the mixture becoming creamy and airy.

10. Transfer to a chilled glass bowl and freeze at freezer temp around minus 15°C. The ice cream will be ready to eat in 5 hours.

• • •

Variations:
  Strawberry ice cream:

1. Chop and puree 200 gm of fresh strawberries. Reduce the milk quantity to 400 ml and follow steps as for vanilla ice cream. Omit the vanilla essence.
2. Add 100 ml of strawberry puree at the time of cream addition.

• • •

Mango Ice cream:

1. Puree 2 medium Alphonso mangoes. Reduce the milk quantity to 400 ml and follow steps as for vanilla ice cream. Omit the vanilla essence.
2. Add 100 ml of mango puree at the time of cream addition.

• • •

Butter scotch ice-cream:

1. Soak and peel 10 almonds. Roast lightly. Chop into small pieces.
2. Caramelise half cup of sugar till golden brown. Add 2 tbsp unsalted butter and add chopped almonds and spread on a parchment paper or aluminium foil.
3. Once it solidifies, then break into small pieces or crush coarsely. Add to the ice cream mixture while churning.

• • •

Chocolate ice cream:

1. To the basic vanilla ice cream recipe, you will require 2/3 cup cocoa, and ½ cup chopped dark chocolate and ½ tsp instant coffee.
2. Add above to the boiling milk and sugar and simmer for 5 minutes. Adjust the sweetness to your taste. Then proceed as for vanilla ice cream.

• • •

Tutti frutti ice cream:

1. Replace the vanilla essence with Tutti frutti essence (Ossoro). Add 4 drops of red/orange colour and proceed as for vanilla ice cream. Towards the end of churning, add ¾ cup of tutti frutti candy.

• • •

Salted caramel ice cream

- 1 ½ cup sugar
- ½ cup water
- 1 cup cream – hot
- 2 tbsp butter
- 1 tsp salt

Method

1. Place sugar and water in a pan. Stir to dissolve the sugar. Heat on high and bring to boil.
2. As soon as the colour is amber, remove from fire.
3. Wearing gloves, slowly pour the hot cream into the caramel and whisk (the mixture will bubble at first and then calm down}. Add the butter and mix. Add salt little by little. Cool.
4. Take half the above caramel sauce. While churning the basic ice cream, mix the caramel in the last one minute of churning. Use the rest of the caramel sauce as a topping.

Mango Mastani

Many years ago during our student days in Pune, we used to visit this small café on Tilak road - Kawre's. And the dinner was pav bhaji with Mango Mastani. In summers, at the peak of Alphonso season, we indulge ourselves in this combination and feel that life is worth living just for this!

Ingredients

- 250 ml cold milk
- 1 cup Alphonso mango pulp
- 4 scoops of mango ice-cream
- ½ cup mango slivers
- 2 tbsp powdered sugar

Method

1. Whip the milk, powdered sugar and mango pulp in the mixie.
2. Divide into 4 tall glasses.
3. Place a scoop of mango ice-cream over the milkshake.
4. Top it with mango slivers.
5. Enjoy with piping hot Pav bhaji.

Chocolate Cake

My friend Indu's recipe for a delicious and easy chocolate cake. We were at Gorakhpur from 1995 to 1998. The kids were small and no decent bakery in town. Birthday parties meant 20 to 30 children all prancing around and we had to do all the catering including making fancy cakes. This chocolate cake can be cut finely without crumbling and moulded into various shapes like butterfly, clock, mickey mouse etc

Ingredients

- 2 eggs
- 1 ¼ cup maida
- 1 ¼ cup sugar
- ¼ cup sunflower oil
- 1 cup curd
- 1 tsp soda
- 1 ½ tbsp cocoa
- ½ tsp vanilla essence

Method

1. Put all the ingredients in the dry grinder of the mixie and run for 3 minutes.
2. The batter will look a little runny.
3. Grease and line a baking tin with parchment paper.
4. Preheat the oven to 180℃.
5. Pour the batter in the tin.
6. Bake at 180℃ for one hour.
7. Let it cool before removing on a tray.

Custard Chocolate Sauce Biscuit Pudding

Another simple recipe from Indu from Gorakhpur days. This is when we had to invent and re-invent dishes based on available ingredients. There are three components to this dish which are assembled together – custard, chocolate sauce and Marie biscuits.

Ingredients

- Marie biscuits 1 pkt 200 gm
- Milk 1 cup

Custard

- 1 litre full cream milk
- 1 tin milkmaid
- 1 tetrapak cream (200 ml)
- 4 tbsp custard powder
- Half cup cold milk

Chocolate sauce

- 1 glass of cold milk
- 8 tsp icing sugar (or 8 tsp powdered sugar plus 1 tbsp cornflour)
- 4 tsp drinking chocolate
- 2 tsp cocoa
- 1 tsp butter
- ½ cup water

Method

1. Empty 1 litre milk in a thick bottomed pan.
2. Add 1 tin of milkmaid.
3. Mix well. Bring to boil
4. Mix custard powder in half a cup of cold milk. Slowly add to the boiling milk mixture on low flame. Stir continuously for 5 minutes.
5. Cool. Then beat in 200 ml of cream till smooth. Keep aside

For Chocolate Sauce

1. Sieve the powders. Add the powders to the rest of the ingredients, blend and boil till slightly thick. Cool.

Assembly

1. Dip each biscuit in milk for 5 seconds and line the serving dish with biscuits.
2. Pour the custard over it.
3. Pour chocolate sauce over it.
4. Repeat the above process.
5. Chill and serve.

Choco Lava Cake

My friend Uma Sridhar, who ironically is not fond of sweets, shared this recipe with me. When had with a scoop of Vanilla ice cream, this dessert transports you to smiling childhood memories.

Ingredients

- 175 gm dark chocolate, grated or chopped
- 125 gm maida
- 150 gm powdered sugar
- 3 eggs
- 125 gm unsalted butter
- Pinch of salt

Method

1. Preheat the oven to 200°C.
2. Use a double boiler method for melting the chocolate. You will need two pots/pans for this. In the bottom pot, fill it with 2 inches of water.
3. Put the grated chocolate and butter in the top pot. This pot should firmly fit over the bottom one.
4. Turn on the gas and keep it on simmer. Slowly stir the chocolate mixture till all the chocolate has melted uniformly and no lumps remain.
5. Put off the gas. Add sugar. Stir well. Cool the chocolate mixture for 2 to 3 minutes.
6. Add the eggs, one at a time, and whisk. Fold in the maida.
7. Grease the ramekins or moulds with butter and dust with maida.
8. Pour the chocolate mixture into moulds filling upto three-fourths. Bake at 200°C for 12 minutes.
9. Invert the moulds/ramekins on a plate and remove the cakes.
10. The choco lava cakes should be cooked on top and have a flowing centre when cut.
11. Serve this immediately with a scoop of vanilla ice cream.

Tips

1. The moulds have to be well greased so that the cakes come out easily.

2. The timing of the baking is important. So do check the oven after 10 minutes to see if the top is done and you may put off the oven.
3. Do not bake in a microwave oven.
4. You could add a square of dark chocolate after pouring the cake batter in the moulds. Press gently so that it is covered with the batter and then bake.

Tiramisu

Mrs. Maria Duckworth shared this delightful fancy dessert with me, including tips. One of most exotic desserts I have made. It comes out really drool worthy and has the WOW factor when served.

This fits a 9 by 9 inches square dish

Ingredients

- 1 packet Savioardi biscuits (lady finger biscuits) – available at department stores or online
- 1 tub Mascaporne cheese (400 gm)
- Half cup Amul cream cheese
- 1 tetrapak (250ml) Amul cream
- 1 tsp Nescafe coffee dissolved in 1 cup boiling water
- Add 3-4 tsp brandy – optional – to the coffee water when cool
- 2 tsp Cocoa

Method

1. Beat Mascarpone, cream and cream cheese over ice. Keep aside.
2. Take the biscuits. Dip in coffee liquid, count till 4 and place in the dish in a single layer.
3. Spread half of the cream mixture over the biscuit layer.
4. Repeat the biscuit layer.
5. Add cream layer on top.
6. Sprinkle sieved cocoa on top.
7. Serve chilled.

Apple Pie

Shortcrust pastry is a useful skill to use and learn. I use the base for apple pie, mango tart etc.

Shortcrust pastry (make 2 of the below pastry, one for base and one for top)

Ingredients

- 200 gm maida
- 100 gm butter chilled
- 2 tsp powdered sugar
- Cold water to bind

Apple stuffing

- 5 medium apples
- 2 tbsp demerara sugar
- 1 tbsp cornflour
- 1 tsp cinnamon powder
- Juice of 1 lime.

Method

1. Dice the cold butter in cubes.
2. Add it to the maida and sugar and rub it in with fingertips till it resembles crumbs and can be brought together.
3. Add cold water and make a dough.
4. Cover with cling film and chill in refrigerator for half an hour.
5. Meanwhile preheat the oven to 180 ℃
6. After half an hour, roll the pastry to fit a 9 inch pie dish. Remove the extra dough from the sides.
7. Prick with a fork.
8. Put an aluminium foil on the pastry. Put some rajma beans on the foil and bake blind for 15 minutes at 180℃ in a preheated oven.
9. Remove from oven. Take out the rajma and tin foil from the shortcrust pastry.

Method (Apple stuffing)

1. Peel and dice the apples. Add the lime juice and rest of ingredients. Place in a sauce pan and cook lightly for 3 minutes.
2. Place the apple filling in the pastry.
3. Roll out another shortcrust pastry, cut in 1 inch strips.
4. Cover the apple filling with the strips in a criss-cross fashion.
5. Bake in a preheated oven at 180°C for 10-15 minutes till it looks light brown. Serve hot.

Chutneys and Sauces

- Tomato Chutney (Bengali style)
- Aamer Chutney
- Coconut Chutney
- Mint Coriander chutney
- Raw Mango and Mint Chutney
- Red Dosa chutney
- Imli Chutney
- Mango Thokku
- Dry Garlic Chutney
- White Sauce

Tomato Chutney (Bengali Style)

Traditionally, Bengalis eat this chutney at the end of the main course, to cleanse the palate and be ready for the Mishti and desserts. However, we are so fond of this chutney that we have it with the meal. Also I pair it with aloo kachori and it's a breakfast treat on special Sundays.

Ingredients

- 250 gm ripe tomatoes – chopped into big chunks
- 1 tsp panch phoran – I mix equal quantities of mustard seeds, jeera, kalonji, fennel seeds ((badi saunf) and half the quantity of methi seeds
- Sugar 2 tbsp
- ¼ tsp salt
- Kismis 1 tbsp
- Ginger – half an inch piece, julienned
- 1 green chilli sliced
- 1 tsp oil

Method

1. Heat the oil. Add the panch phoran and let it cook for a minute.
2. Add the tomatoes, ginger and green chilli. Cook covered for 2-3 minutes.
3. Add the sugar and salt.
4. Add half a cup of water and bring to a boil. Add the kismis.
5. Reduce the flame to medium and cook covered till the tomatoes are done.
6. Remove the lid and cook till the mixture is thick in consistency.
7. Check the salt and sugar.
8. Cool and store in the refrigerator for 3-4 days.

Aamer Chutney (Bengali raw mango chutney)

This is very similar to the Bengali Tomato chutney and is regularly made in summers.

Ingredients

- 3 raw mangoes- chopped into big chunks
- 1 tsp panch phoran (see tomato chutney for the panch phoran mix)
- ½ tsp haldi
- ½ tsp salt
- 3 tbsp sugar
- 1 red chilli
- 1 tsp oil
- 2 tbsp raisins

Method

1. Roast the panch phoran for 1 minute. Grind coarsely.
2. Heat the oil in a pan.
3. Add the red chilli and fry for half a minute.
4. Add haldi and the chopped mangoes and mix well.
5. Cover the pan and cook for 5 minutes, stirring in between.
6. Add the sugar, salt and raisins.
7. Cook covered till the mangoes are soft. If it appears dry, then add 2-3 tbsp of water.
8. Remove from the flame.
9. Add the ground panch phoran and mix well.
10. This can be refrigerated for 5 days.

Coconut Chutney

A little heat doesn't hurt. I make this dosa-idli chutney slightly spicy to add a zing to my breakfast.

Ingredients:

- 1 cup coconut grated
- Half cup roasted channa dal (chutney dal)
- ¼ inch ginger chopped
- 2 green chillies chopped
- Salt to taste
- Half tsp sugar
- Grind the above in a small grinder with water. The consistency should be thick.

Tempering:

- 1 tsp oil
- Half tsp mustard seeds
- 8 curry leaves
- 1 red chilli broken

Method

1. Heat oil. Add above. Cook for a minute and pour it in the ground chutney.
2. Serve with dosa, idli, vada, utthappam.

Coconut Coriander Chutney

Ingredients:

- 1 cup coconut grated
- ¼ cup chopped coriander leaves
- ½ cup roasted channa dal (chutney dal)
- ¼ inch ginger chopped
- 2 green chillies chopped
- Salt to taste, ½ tsp sugar
- Grind the above in a small grinder with water. The consistency should be thick.

Tempering:

- 1 tsp oil
- Half tsp mustard seeds
- 8 curry leaves

Method

1. Heat oil. Add above. Cook for a minute and pour it in the ground chutney. Serve with rava idli.

Note: If using grated coconut which has been frozen or refrigerated, grind using hot water so that the oil doesn't separate.

Mint Coriander Chutney

Mint Coriander Chutney -1
A must have chutney for chaats, pakodas or simply to add a zesty feel to a meal.

Ingredients

- 1 cup pudina leaves
- 2 cups dhania leaves chopped
- 2 green chillies
- 2 tbsp spring onion- both leaves and whites. If not available, use half a small onion chopped
- 1 tbsp nimbu juice
- Salt to taste
- Half tsp sugar

Method

1. Grind all above except the nimbu juice. Once finely ground, add the nimbu juice.
2. Taste and adjust salt and add more nimbu juice if required.

• • •

Mint Coriander Chutney -2
Pudina chutney (courtesy Mrs. Meenaxi Bhatt, whose hospitality for dishes from Uttarakhand is legendary)

Ingredients

- 1 cup pudina leaves
- 2 cups dhania leaves
- 2 medium tomatoes
- Imli marble size, soaked in 2 tbsp water
- 1 green chilli
- 1 tsp jeera
- Salt to taste

Method

1. Squeeze out the pulp from the imli. Grind all the ingredients to a fine paste. It should not be too thick.
2. Serve with parathas.

Tip

1. Use only pudina leaves, not stems. For coriander, use leaves and tender stalks.

Raw Mango and Mint Chutney

Summer time is raw mango time. I try and use it in as many recipes as possible.

Ingredients:

- 1 medium raw mango- peeled and chopped
- Half cup fresh mint (pudina) leaves
- 1 cup chopped coriander leaves
- 2 green chillies - chopped
- Salt to taste
- Half tsp sugar

Method:

1. In a small grinder, first grind the mango till no lumps remain.
2. Add the rest of the ingredients with 2 tsp water and grind well.
3. Store in refrigerator.
4. It keeps well for 3-4 days.

Tips

1. Chillies can be adjusted as per spice requirement.
2. If the mango is very sour, a little more sugar can be added.
3. I like thick chutneys. However, you may increase the water to achieve the desired consistency.

Red Dosa Chutney

Dr. Neelamani Murthy taught me this delightful chutney to elevate the dosa eating experience to a different level.

Ingredients (for 1 cup chutney)

- 1 big onion chopped
- 2 big tomatoes chopped
- 2 -3 red chillies broken
- 2 tsp urad dal
- 2 tsp channa dal
- Salt to taste
- 2 tsp oil
- Hing a pinch
- ½ tsp methi seeds

Method

1. Heat the oil in a pan.
2. Add methi seeds, hing and red chilli. Add both the dals. Sauté till the dals turn golden.
3. Add the onions. Sauté till the onion is translucent.
4. Add the tomatoes. Cook till pulpy. Add the salt.
5. Cool.
6. Grind in a small grinder till you get a smooth chutney.

Tip

1. I use Bydagi red chillies. These are not hot but impart a beautiful red colour.

Thokku

Mango Thokku

I love this grated mango delicacy - tangy and spicy, especially during the summers. Thanks to Deepa Rajagopal, I've managed to recreate it just as my mom would have made for us.

Ingredients:

- Big raw mangoes – peeled and grated (3 cups of grated mango)
- ½ tsp haldi
- 1 tsp salt
- 2 tsp methi (fenugreek) seeds – roasted and ground
- 2 tbsp chilli powder
- ½ tsp hing
- 1 tsp mustard seeds
- Half a cup oil

Method:

1. Heat oil.
2. Add mustard seeds and fry till they crackle.
3. Add mangoes, haldi, salt, and red chilli powder. Cook, stirring often until all the water has evaporated.
4. Add methi powder and hing. Check salt and spice seasoning.
5. Stir for 10 minutes till oil leaves the side of the pan.
6. Cool. Store refrigerated for up to a week.
7. Serve as a side accompaniment to a typical south Indian meal.

• • •

Tomato Thokku

1. The preparation is very similar to the mango thokku.
2. In lieu of raw mangoes, use 5-6 ripe medium sized tomatoes. Dice the tomatoes.
3. Then proceed as for mango thokku adding 5-6 curry leaves in the tempering.

Dry Garlic Chutney

A Maharashtrian accompaniment not only to batata vada but as a side to a daily meal. This recipe is from my mother-in-law whose chutney is relished by my younger daughter Shivani.

Ingredients:

- 2 cups grated copra (dry coconut)
- ½ cup peeled garlic cloves (preferably of the same size)
- 2 tbsp red chilli powder
- 1 tsp Amchur
- Salt to taste
- 1 tsp oil

Method:

1. Heat the oil in a pan.
2. Fry the garlic till they turn light brown, but do not burn. Remove the garlic and chop coarsely.
3. In the same oil, sauté the copra till light brown – just requires a minute.
4. Cool
5. Combine the garlic, copra, salt, amchur and red chilli powder and grind coarsely.

White Sauce (Béchamel Sauce)

I use this sauce for baked spinach corn, baked vegetables, and pasta. It is easy to make with everyday staples from the pantry.

Ingredients:

- Milk 1 cup (200 ml)
- 1 tbsp maida
- 1 tbsp butter
- ¼ tsp salt
- ¼ tsp pepper powder
- Pinch of nutmeg powder

Method:

1. In a heavy bottomed or nonstick frying pan, melt the butter. Add the maida and keep stirring for around 2-3 minutes on low flame. The maida should not turn brown.
2. Put off the gas and remove the pan from the stove. Let it cool slightly.
3. Warm the milk. Gradually whisk the milk into the maida-butter mixture. Whisk well till there are no lumps. Place the pan back on heat.
4. Add the salt, pepper and nutmeg and keep stirring over low flame till you get a thick smooth consistency. This would take 4-5 minutes.
5. Adjust salt and pepper as per taste.

Tips:

1. The milk should be warm. If you use cold milk, then lumps will form.
2. The key moment is firstly to make the butter-maida mixture on a low flame. Do not hurry.
3. Also the milk and maida mixture should be at the same warm temperature. Stir slowly, avoid lumps. Only when it is smooth, bring it back on the gas and continue to cook over low flame, till it becomes a nice creamy mixture. You may add more milk to achieve the necessary consistency.
4. You could use this sauce as a base for pasta. You may add cheese or cream to make it rich.

Useful Tips

- **Groundnut powder:** Roast around a cupful of peanuts on low flame. Peel them by rubbing with the hands. Then grind them coarsely. This is always there in my pantry.
- **Powdered sugar:** another useful handy item to have. I use it for nimbu pani, salads. The sugar dissolves much quicker than granulated sugar.
- **Dosa and idli batters:** After grinding, make the batter to the correct consistency and then ferment. After use, store the remaining batter in the refrigerator. Thaw it and use. This way the bubbles remain and you don't have to dilute it further.
- **Grated coconut:** I keep grated coconut in the freezer and thaw only how much I need.
- **Coconut chutney:** In case you are using frozen grated coconut for chutney, then use hot water for grinding the chutney. This prevents the coconut butter from forming.
- **Making curd (dahi):** It sounds simple, but with so many different seasons, I keep modifying my technique. For half litre milk, I use 2 tsp of curd for setting. Mix the curd well and stir it in warm milk. Keep in a warm place for 6-8 hours or overnight. This works well in summers. However, in winter season, I either cover the bowl with a warm cloth like shawl and then set it, or place the bowl in a casserole. The milk also has to be slightly more warmer in winter before mixing the curd.
- **Bydagi chillies:** I use Bydagi red chillies, which are available from Karnataka. It is similar to Kashmiri red chillies – it gives the colour but not the heat.
- **Eggs storage:** store eggs with the pointed side facing down. The air sac is at the broader end and allows exchange of gases. This was suggested by Dr. Sanjay Bhargava and it works.
- **Masala powders:** Those masalas that I don't use very often, I store them in the freezer compartment. This way, the flavors are retained for a longer time. I learnt this from Mrs. Kang.
- **Store bought powders:** I use some store bought powders for my cooking. Especially the dishes I do not make often. Like Bisibele bhath powder, Puliyogare powder-both from MTR. Pav bhaji masala from Everest. This does make life easier.
- I use only Ossoro French vanilla essence for ice-creams and fruit yoghurt. It is very light and not overpowering.
- **Weighing scale:** an absolute essential for baking purposes.
- Measuring cups and spoons are also essential. The cup mentioned in this book holds 200 ml.

Glossary

ENGLISH	HINDI
Spices	
Cumin	Jeera
Coriander	Dhania
Fenugreek	Methi
Mustard	Rai
Nigella seeds	Kalonji
Fennel seeds	Saunf
Clove	Lavang
Cinnamon	Dalchini
Cardamom	Elaichi
Carom seeds	Ajwain
Bay leaf	Tej patta
Mace	Javitri
Nutmeg	Jaiphal
Black pepper	Kali mirch
Red chilli	Lal mirchi
Turmeric	Haldi
Asafoetida	Hing
Raw mango powder	Amchur
Black salt	Kala namak
Dried gooseberry	Amla
Dried fenugreek leaves	Kasoori Methi
Lentils	
Pigeon pea	Arhar or tur dal
Roasted Bengal Gram	Chutney dal
Chickpeas	Kabuli channa / chole
Green Gram	Moong dal
Red lentil	Masoor dal
Bengal Gram	Channa dal
Black Gram	Urad dal
Black eyed beans	Lobia
Kidney beans	Rajma
Black chickpeas	Kala Chana
Flours	
Whole wheat flour	Atta
Refined flour	Maida
Semolina	Sooji / rava
Sorghum flour	Jowar
Vermicelli	Seviyan

Rice flour	Chawal ka atta
Chickpea flour	Besan
Flattened rice	Poha
Sago	Sabudana
Puffed rice	Murmura
Peanut / groundnut	Moongphali
Coconut	Narial
Coconut dry	Copra
Vegetables	
Okra / lady's finger	Bhindi
Brinjal / Aubergine	Baingan
Radish	Mooli
Beetroot	Chukandar
Cabbage	Pattagobi
Cauliflower	Phool Gobi
Chayote squash	Chow chow
Cucumber	Kheera
Ginger	Adrak
Garlic	Lasun
Potato	Aloo
Onion	Pyaaz
Capsicum	Simla Mirchi
Lime/ lemon	Nimbu
Curry leaves	Kadipatta
Coriander leaves	Dhania patta
Fenugreek leaves	Methi patta
Spinach	Palak
Mint	Pudina
Mustard leaves	Sarson ka saag
Others	
Sesame seeds	Til
Jaggery	Gud
Raisins	Kismis
Cashewnut	Kaju
Almond	Badam
Dates	Khajur
Saffron	Kesar
Curd / yoghurt	Dahi
Tamarind	Imli
Miscellaneous	
Tempering	Tadka
Frying pan	Kadhai
Griddle	Tawa

Made in United States
North Haven, CT
21 November 2024

60662166R00119